The
Dambusters
Squadron

Fifty Years of 617 Squadron RAF

The Dambusters Squadron

Fifty Years of 617 Squadron RAF

Alan Cooper

ARMS AND
ARMOUR

*The Dambusters at Buckingham
Palace in June 1943: Sumpter,
Taerum, Spafford, Buckley,
Martin, Maltby, Gibson, Johnson,
Shannon, McCarthy, Franklin
(recipient of the only ever bar to
DFM in 617's history) Fort,
Wilkinson, Chambers and
Chalmers. (Author)*

Arms and Armour Press
A Cassell Imprint
Villiers House, 41-47 Strand, London WC2N 5JE.

Distributed in the USA by Sterling Publishing Co. Inc., 387 Park Avenue South, New York, NY 10016-8810.

Distributed in Australia by Capricorn Link (Australia) Pty. Ltd, P.O. Box 665, Lane Cove, New South Wales 2066.

British Library Cataloguing-in-Publication Data: a catalogue record for this book is available from the British Library

ISBN 1-85409-182-4

Designed and edited by DAG Publications Ltd. Designed by David Gibbons; edited by Michael Boxall; layout by Anthony A. Evans; camerawork by M&E Reproductions, North Fambridge, Essex; printed and bound in Great Britain by The Bath Press, Avon.

Other books by Alan Cooper:

The Men who Breached the Dams
Beyond the Dams to the Tirpitz
Bombers over Berlin
In Action with the Enemy
Free to Fight Again
The Air Battle of the Ruhr

Acknowledgements
Her Majesty The Queen Mother
Joachim W. Ziegler
617 Squadron RAF Marham
Betty Pike
Public Record Office
Air Historical Branch
Royal Library Windsor
Royal Air Force News
Mark Upton
Bill Howarth, DFM
Dr Ursula Wolkers
Colin Wallwork
Einar Hovding
MOD — PMC Innsworth
Group Captain Ned Frith, CBE, AFC
AVM Douglas Bower, CBE, AFC
Bob Knights, DSO, DFC
Edward Wass
Gerald Preece
Horst Muller
Einar Harding
ACM Sir Michael Bearis, KCB, CBE, AFC
Wing Commander Bob Iveson MID
Flight Lieutenant Mark Jones
Flight Lieutenant Gareth Walker
Flight Lieutenant Paul Wharmby
Flight Lieutenant Richard Crook
Flight Lieutenant Mark Youngman
Corporal John Evans
Corporal Paul Vickers
Junior Technician Paul Fullalove
Flying Officer Becky Colbourne, WRAF
T. Wass 617 Squadron Association
G. A. Coombe
All the staff of 617 Squadron for their hospitality during my visit to them at Marham
Carol Andrews for her excellent advice and typing skills
My wife Hilda for her support and advice whenever called upon

Contents

I am delighted to have been invited to write a Foreword for this book which marks the 50th Anniversary of the formation of 617 Squadron - The Dambusters - Royal Air Force.

From the time of its formation The King took a very keen interest in the Squadron, an interest which I shared and have retained to this day.

Shortly after the raid on the Ruhr Dams - an operation of superb skill and infinite bravery which was an inspiration to the Allied forces, I accompanied The King when he visited the Squadron at RAF Scampton. It was later my pleasure, in the absence of His Majesty in Algiers, to hold the Investiture in June 1943 when thirty-four members of the Squadron, including Wing Commander Guy Gibson VC, received Decorations for outstanding gallantry.

Since then I have been happy to maintain my connection with 617 Squadron by twice presenting new standards and have thus been able to continue an association which started some fifty years ago in the dark days of World War II.

ELIZABETH R
Queen Mother

1992

Left and below left: A bouncing bomb at the Breznett Aviation Museum near Folkestone, Kent. This bomb was recovered from Reculver Bay where trials of the weapon were conducted in 1943. (G. Shoesmith)

Introduction

Fifty years ago 133 men in nineteen aircraft of 617 Squadron RAF set out on an operation that was to become legendary in the annals of the RAF and the Second World War. The object was the destruction of the German Moehne and Eder dams in the Ruhr. Many who know little about the war will have heard of The Dambusters, but perhaps not know who they were or that their Squadron, 617, is still very much active in 1992.

It is twenty years since I first became interested in the raid on the Ruhr dams. Since then the 50-year-old operation has become an important part of my life. My interest led me to write a book — *The Men who Breached the Dams* — the story of the men who undertook the operation, and of those 56 who failed to return. I then began to look further into the history of 617 Squadron and its subsequent post-dams operations, such as the sinking of the German battleship *Tirpitz* and the use of Tallboy and Grand Slam super bombs.

From this came a second book: *Beyond the Dams to the Tirpitz*. And now this book completes the fifty-year history of 617, and includes the recent Gulf War in which crews from 617 Squadron played a prominent part in the Tornado force. The spirit of these men is the same as that of fifty years ago; only the aircraft and the technology have changed. The usual aircrew banter of old is always evident but behind it is an intense dedication and awareness that the job of flying such aircraft as the Tornado at great speeds and at low level is a very exacting and dangerous occupation. There is little room for error and the job does not suffer fools gladly.

During my twenty years of research on 617 I have had the great privilege and pleasure of meeting many outstanding and unique men who have served in the RAF, and others who contributed to its success: Sir Arthur Harris, Commander-in-Chief, Bomber Command; The Hon Ralph Cochrane, AOC No 5 Group and Don Bennett, the wartime Pathfinder Group Commander to name but three. Above all the incomparable Dr Barnes Wallis with whom I spent two memorable days and had the great honour of taking the last known photograph of him. He, of course, was the man responsible for the design of the two largest conventional bombs used during the war; but he was to an intense degree a man of peace, whose greatest frustration was the futility of war; his skills were used only to bring it to an end as soon as possible.

On the German side a visit to Heidelberg and the home of Dr Albert Speer, the wartime Armaments Minister, enabled me to share his thoughts and memories which are a testament to the efforts and contribution that Bomber Command had in ending the war in Europe.

I am often asked and I am sure will continue to be asked what effect the breaching of the dams had on the war. There is no easy answer to this question, if in hindsight it is possible to answer it at all, but I am certain that it played its part in the Battle of the Ruhr in 1943 in depriving the Germans of resources required to sustain the war effort. In so doing it also helped speed the war's end. There is no doubt that the raid was of enormous psychological value in boosting the morale of the public in the United Kingdom and, more importantly, of the RAF at a time when this was urgently needed. Today we can see that the men of 617 are keeping up the traditions and reputation of the Squadron, and it is fitting that their exploits be discussed in a book embracing the full fifty years of their history as a squadron rather than fragmented into different periods. They are a front-line fighting unit and are ready to face whatever challenge is presented to them, as demonstrated in the Gulf War. Theirs is a squadron with a charisma of its own, which I hope will become apparent to the reader.

Left: Another bouncing bomb that was recovered from Reculver and is now kept at the Imperial War Museum's section at Duxford. (Author)

Left: A model dam built in secret at Garston in 1940 for testing the explosive charge needed for 'Chastise'. The effects of the tests can still be seen.

The Squadron is Formed

'X' Squadron RAF Bomber Command was formed on 18 March 1943, its role being to attack and destroy the Moehne, Sorpe and Eder dams in Germany's industrial heartland, the Ruhr. The Squadron became formally known as 617 Squadron on 24 March 1943.

The Squadron was to use a specially designed new weapon, officially known as a mine, bomb or store. Having been made to rotate at 500 revolutions per minute while still in its carrier aboard the aircraft, it would be released from a height of 60 feet 400 yards from the dam and would skip across the surface of the water. On striking the face of the dam it would sink to a depth of 30 feet where it would be exploded by a pre-set time/hydrostatic fuze.

Twenty-one aircraft and 147 aircrew were posted in from main force squadrons throughout Lincolnshire, all from No 5 Group Bomber Command. The man chosen to command the Squadron and lead the operation was Wing Commander Guy Gibson, DSO, DFC: an able and experienced pilot with more than 100 operations in his logbook.

At this time Bomber Command was still testing its own and the enemy's strength in the initial raids of the hardfought Battle of the Ruhr. Although costly and not without its critics, the offensive was to continue until the end of the war, and contribute vitally to victory. The attack on the dams, although a one-off operation, was part of the overall plan to destroy the German armaments industry in the Ruhr since it was believed that the breaching of the dams would deprive the Germans of water and electricity needed in many manufacturing processes: one ton of steel, for example, required 10,000 tons of water in its manufacture.

The operational code-name for the attack was 'Chastise' and that for the special weapon was 'Upkeep'. To carry the bomb the Avro Lancaster heavy bomber, then coming into front-line service, needed much special adaptation including the removal of bomb bay doors and modification of the underside of the fuselage. Two external carrier arms were fitted, one on each side of the fuselage, and the normal saucer-shaped transparent moulding of the

bomb-aimer's window was replaced by one of almost hemispherical shape.

There followed more than seven weeks of intensive training as the aircrew of 617 Squadron mastered the difficult art of precision navigation while flying at very low altitude; none of them knew any details of the forthcoming operation. Not surprisingly inexperience and the pressure of discovering problems for themselves raised many difficulties.

The most difficult problem was that of maintaining a height of exactly 60 feet over water at night, but the solution was as simple as it was effective. Ted Calvert, an illumination expert at the Royal Aircraft Establishment, who had been approached by Ben Lockspier at the Ministry of Aircraft Production, perfected a First World War idea of mounting two spotlights, one beneath the tail and the other beneath the nose of the aircraft. When angled appropriately the two beams converged to form a single circle of light on the surface 60 feet below.

Unusually for a Bomber Command raid, 'Chastise' would employ a Master Bomber to monitor progress and talk each aircraft on to the target. This required the installation of VHF radios in the Lancasters, similar to those used in Fighter Command, and the normal Type TR1196 was replaced by the VHF Type TR1143. Once these were working properly and the crews had been trained in their use under No 5 Group Signals Officer, Wing Commander Wally Dunn, reception during tests was found to be good.

The Squadron would need all available assistance available because the targets were formidable. The Moehne dam was 105 feet high, more than 2,000 feet long and 112 feet thick at its base, narrowing to 25 feet at the crest. It was protected by two parallel rows of anti-torpedo netting supported from floating wooden booms which stretched nearly 300 feet out across the water. It was defended by numerous anti-aircraft guns positioned on the crest and in the surrounding hills.

At 58 feet the Sorpe dam was less than half the height of the Moehne. Its construction was slightly different, having a concrete core surrounded by built-up earth and stone, and it was thought that this would make it almost unbreachable.

The third target, the Eder dam in the western Ruhr, was of masonry construction, 139 feet high and 1,300 feet long. It was 45 feet thick at the base, tapering to 19 feet at the crest.

The last of the dams were the Ennepe at 45 feet high and the Lister, 35 feet high. Each main dam was allocated a code-letter to be used in all communications: the dams' actual names and locations, although known to Gibson, remained secret to his crews who had yet to learn about 'X' Moehne, 'Y' Eder and 'Z' Sorpe.

Left: Wing Commander Guy Gibson and Eve Moore's wedding at Penarth in South Wales in 1941. His father Alexander is second right.

Below: Guy Gibson's Dambuster Lancaster G-George at Scampton two days after the dams raid. (Crown Copyright)

Above: *Flight Sergeant Bill Townsend's Lancaster ED866-O photographed by Micky Martin's tail gunner, Tammy Simpson. Note that the bomb has been released.*

Right: *Gibson's G-George after the dams raid. The mechanism for holding the bomb and the belt drive that rotated it prior to release are clearly visible. (Crown Copyright)*

Above: The Moehne dam before the attack. *(Author)*

Right: The Eder dam in 1980. Note in the extreme left-hand corner that the porthole was not replaced during the repairs made in 1943. *(Author)*

Below: The Sorpe in 1980. Note the long stretch of grass-covered earth which made it a difficult target to breach. Both McCarthy and Brown attacked the Sorpe. *(Horst Muller)*

Above: The defences around the Moehne dam after the attack. (Karl Schutte)

Left: The Ennepe dam in 1980. This was a much smaller dam, quite unlike the Moehne or Eder, and was attacked by Townsend. (Horst Muller)

The Raid

The date set for the dams attack was 16 May 1943. Operation code-words were nominated for all targets: 'Goner' would indicate that a bomb had been dropped; 'Nigger' that the Moehne had been breached. This was the name of Gibson's dog who was run over and killed at RAF Scampton on the day before the raid. The code-word for a success at the Eder was 'Dinghy', possibly after 'Dinghy' Young who was one of the flight commanders on the operation. The last code-word was 'Zebra' for the Sorpe. All crew transmissions to base would use the call-sign 'WB1'.

It was fine and sunny on 16 May when the aircrew were summoned to the large dining-room at Scampton. Two crews were reported ill and so the operation was set for nineteen Lancasters and 133 men. Only now was the target revealed to the crews as they saw photographs and models of the dams made at RAF Medmenham. The aircrew were split into three groups, the first of which would number nine Lancasters led by Gibson. They would take off in flights of three aircraft at ten-minute intervals and proceed directly to the Moehne which they would attack until it was breached. This done, any aircraft with its bomb still aboard would proceed to the Eder. If both Eder and Moehne were breached, any remaining bombs would be dropped on the Sorpe.

The second group, 'B' Flight's six aircrew, commanded by Flight Lieutenant Joe McCarthy, would fly directly to the Sorpe and drop their bombs alongside the face of the dam instead of bouncing them across the water.

The third (reserve) group of five aircraft would stand by awaiting the outcome of the Moehne and Eder attacks.

Operation orders stipulated flight at 1,500 feet over England, dropping to 60 feet across the Channel to set altimeters. Final reconnaissance flights had revealed torpedo defences in place at the Moehne and 76mm gun emplacements on its northern banks. On the dam itself were three or four AA guns in two towers at each end of the wall. As briefing continued the nineteen Lancasters were being bombed and fuelled up, a task that occupied 1,500 ground personnel.

At 5 Group HQ in Grantham preparations were also well advanced with Group Signals Officer Wing Commander Wally Dunn preparing to receive all transmissions from the attack force. Regular staff soon realized that a special mission was imminent as Air Chief Marshal Arthur Harris, CinC Bomber Command and AOC No 5 Group, Air Vice Marshal Ralph Cochrane were both present. Also present was a civilian with thick white hair — Dr Barnes Wallis, who had invented the 'bouncing' bomb.

At RAF Scampton Gibson asked Flight Sergeant 'Chiefy' Powell to bury Nigger at midnight, approximately the time he would be over the target area and hoping to transmit the success signal. From 2030 the crews arrived at their aircraft and observed the common rituals of a last cigarette or relieving themselves against the tail wheel of their aircraft. (This was later found to accelerate metal fatigue and the practice was banned.)

Those crews detailed to attack the Sorpe took off first, without Squadron Leader McCarthy who had problems including having to change aircraft and having his parachute open while getting aboard: he eventually took off a full 30 minutes late. Gibson meanwhile took off at 2139 and by 2200 all his aircraft were on course for the Moehne. Arriving first at 0015, Gibson bombed at 0028 but his bomb failed to strike the dam wall dead centre. Thirty minutes later he reported that he had dropped his bomb. Three more aircraft attacked and suddenly the whole dam wall seemed to roll over. The Morse at HQ sounded for the third time, followed by Dunn shouting 'Nigger!'. Relief and excitement was felt by all present, not least by Wallis; against all critics he had persevered and been proven right. Everyone wanted to congratulate him and shake his hand.

Gibson circled the breached dam, surveying the chaos as millions of gallons of water cascaded down the Ruhr valley, and then led the remaining aircraft on to the Eder. Those crews that had attacked already were sent back to Scampton. Although undefended the Eder was a difficult dam to attack; it took Gibson five runs before he located it and was confident enough to fire the marker flare for the others to attack. As at the Moehne, the first bomb exploded beyond the dam wall but the second successfully breached the dam, and the third Lancaster widened the breach to 30 feet. They flew off at 0152 leaving a spume of water from Eder 800 feet high. The remaining aircraft attacked the Sorpe but inflicted only minor damage and although Flight Sergeant Townsend bravely attacked the Ennepe alone, his direct hit caused minimal damage only and he too flew home.

All surviving crews arrived back at Scampton to be met by the AOC and CinC who remained with them throughout the debriefing. Congratulations were later sent by Harris and the War Cabinet but the crew reaction was typically selfless, seeking only to praise the man who had invented the bomb and the many people who had made it all work.

Right: *Nigger's grave outside No 2 hangar at Scampton, just as Chiefy Powell buried him in 1943. (Author)*

Below: *Model of the Sorpe used at the briefing. It is now in the Imperial War Museum. (IWM)*

Above: The model of the Moehne dam is also in the Imperial War Museum. (IWM)

Below: This painting of the attack on the Sorpe shows clearly the method of bombing this dam, by flying across it rather than by bouncing the bomb up to the dam face. (Maurice Gardner)

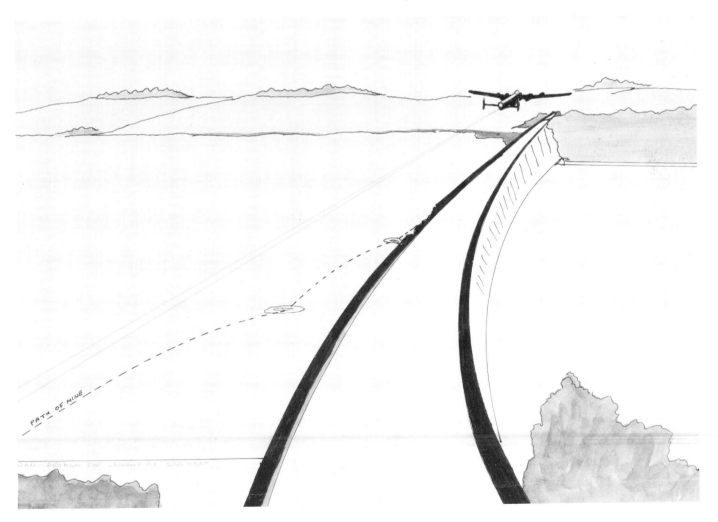

Left: The anti-aircraft guns at the Moehne which shot down John Hopgood as he attacked. (Karl Schutte)

Right: Wing Commander Dunn revisits No 5 Group HQ at Grantham. It was here that he received the signal 'Nigger', indicating that the Moehne dam had been breached. (Wally Dunn)

Left: A different view of the Moehne's anti-aircraft defences. (Karl Schutte)

Right: An oil painting of Arthur Harris, now at the RAF Museum Hendon after years in storage. (PRO)

Far right: Ralph Cochrane, wartime commander of No 5 Group. (IWM)

Left: Dr Barnes Wallis at his desk. Behind him is the large framed photograph of the Moehne dam presented to him on 22 June 1943 by the directors of A.V. Roe at the dams celebration dinner in London. (IWM)

Below Left: George 'Chiefy' Powell who served with 617 Squadron from its formation and was largely responsible for putting the squadron together so quickly. It was he who buried Nigger. When Gibson returned from the raid he presented Powell with the key that fuzed the bomb. (G. Powell)

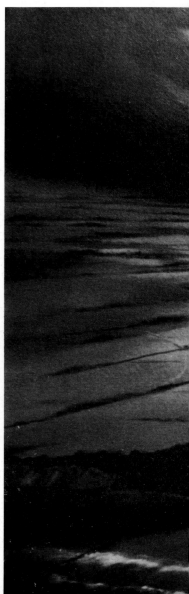

Right: *The operational map showing planned routes of the individual aircraft to and from the dams, each marked by letter. (Author)*

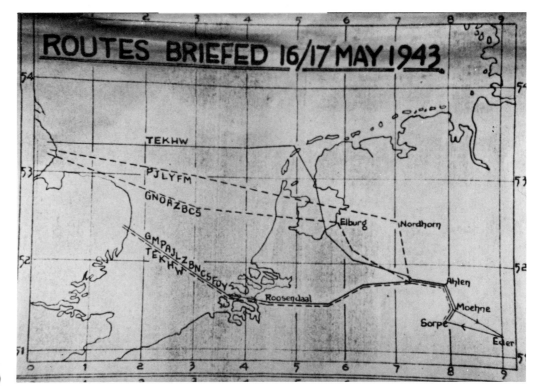

Below: *A painting of ED 886 O-Orange, flown by Flight Sergeant Townsend, en route for the Ennepe. (Painting by Maurice Gardner in the Hayler Collection)*

Details of the special bouncing bomb installation in the Lancasters of 617 Squadron.

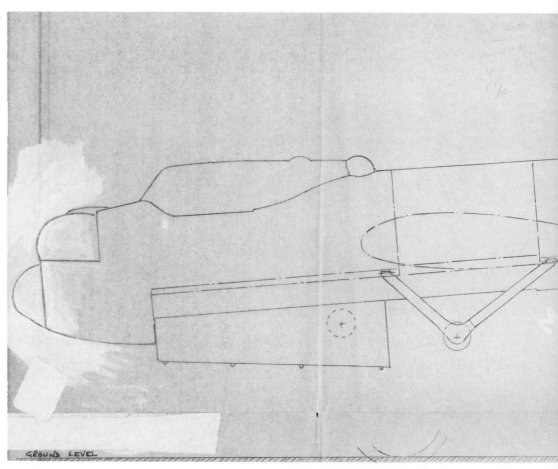

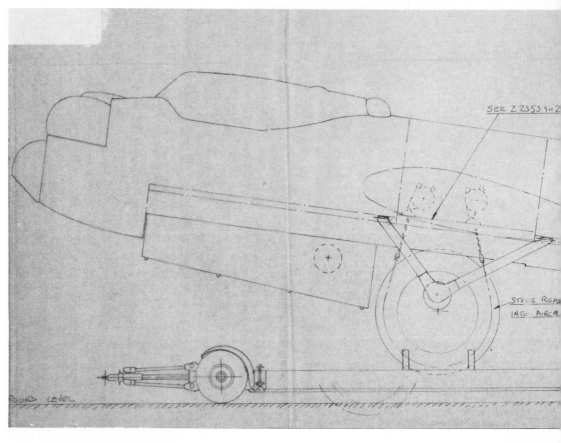

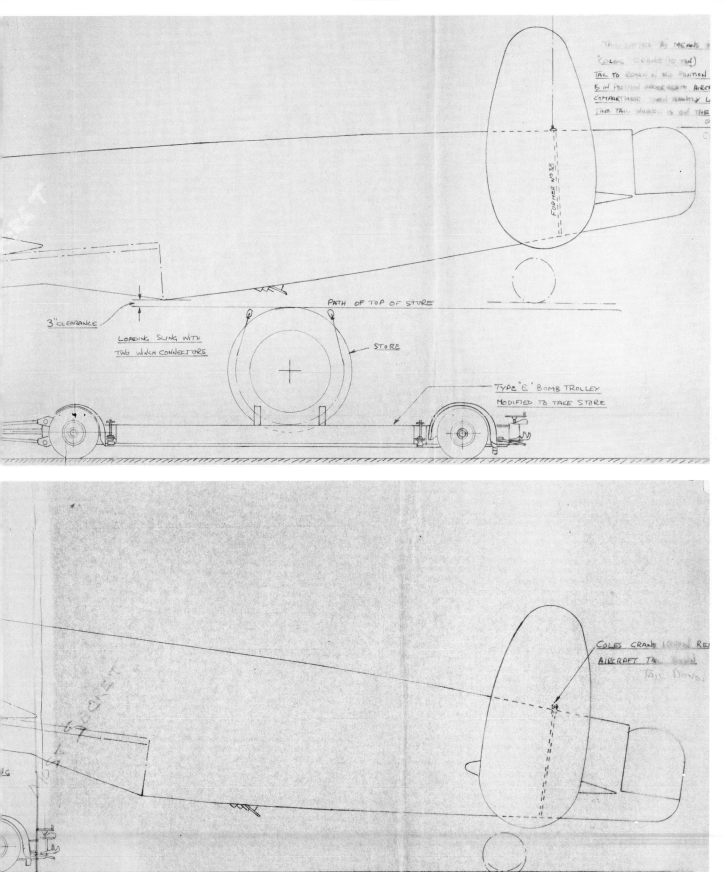

Details of the special bouncing bomb installation in the Lancasters of 617 Squadron.

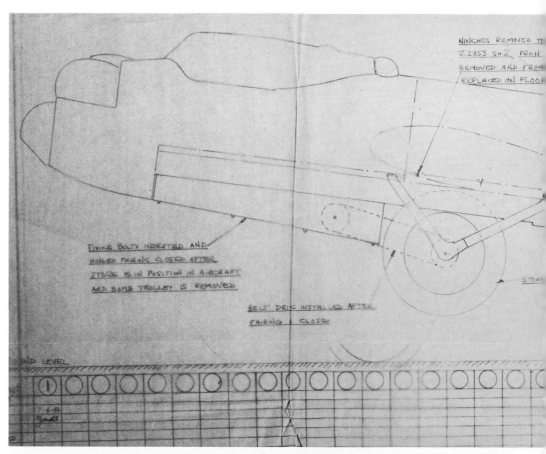

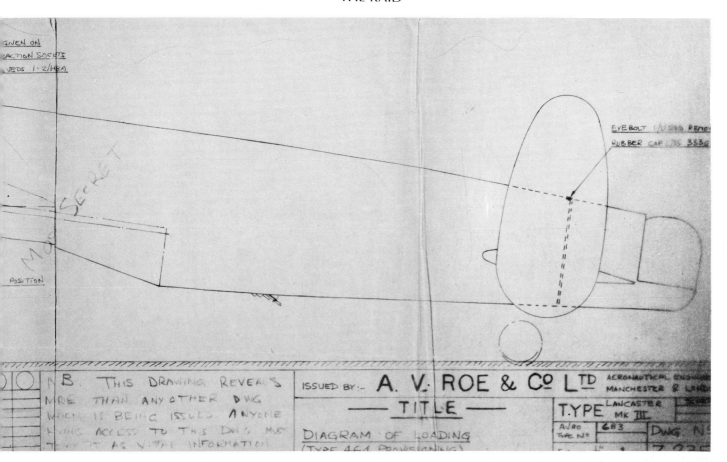

GIVEN ON
ACTION SOCKETS
NEDS 1·2/HBA

EYEBOLT 1/USED REMOV
RUBBER CAP 3338

MOST SECRET

POSITION

	NB. THIS DRAWING REVEALS MORE THAN ANY OTHER DWG WHICH IS BEING ISSUED. ANYONE HAVING ACCESS TO THIS DWG MUST ....T AS VITAL INFORMATION	ISSUED BY :- A. V. ROE & CO LTD	AERONAUTICAL ENG... MANCHESTER & LOND...
		── TITLE ──	TYPE LANCASTER MK III
		DIAGRAM OF LOADING (TYPE 464 PROVISIONING)	AVRO TYPE No 683 DWG. N...

Left: *Guy Gibson's crew being debriefed. Left to right: Harris, Spafford, Cochrane, Taerum and rear-gunner Trevor-Roper. (IWM)*

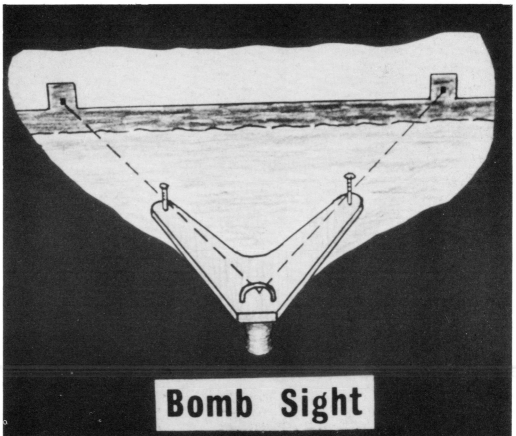

Bomb Sight

Right: *The wooden bombsight used by a number of the bomb-aimers to ensure they were at the right distance from the dam. (Bill Howarth)*

Left: Dr Albert Speer visits the Moehne dam in September 1943 to inspect the repairs to the breach. Because there were no follow-up raids the work was completed in a matter of months. (Horst Muller)

Left: The Moehne after the raid. In the foreground the huge pipes are all that remained of the power station after Hopgood's bomb hit. (Karl Schutte)

Below Left: The rushing waters unleashed from the Moehne. (Horst Muller)

Below: A view from the Moehne of the devastation, taken on the morning after the raid. (Karl Schutte)

Aftermath

The devastation in the immediate area around the dams was colossal; the prime objective, the loss of millions of gallons of vital water, had been achieved. An early morning photo-reconnaissance clearly illustrated more than eighteen miles of the Moehne valley flooded and more than twenty miles in the Eder region. The Sorpe had been damaged and spillage was detected indicating a serious leakage. At the Ennepe only one bomb had been sufficient to weaken the dam and again spillage was seen.

On the morning of the raid the Moehne had held 132 million cubic feet of water: two days later this was down to 14 million cubic feet. The Germans reported a gap 240 feet wide and 70 feet deep and when Armaments Minister Albert Speer visited the area next day he was: '...quite shaken; I could not imagine water could destroy everything. It was far worse than I expected.' Speer estimated that it would require the efforts of 7,000 workers to repair the damage, and of course these workers from the Todt Organization could ill be spared from the Atlantic Wall. His immediate report to Hitler ordered increased anti-aircraft defences at all major dams in Germany — again reducing manpower and resources from other fronts. The effects of the raid give some indication of the tidal wave of destruction that 617 unleashed that night. The late bomb that bounced over the dam destroyed the Moehne power station and severed all electricity supplies to the whole valley; a week later the waters had reached Holland and Belgium more than 100 miles away, sweeping away countless bridges and embankments en route; all main railway lines running east from the Ruhr to Kassel via Schwerte and Frondenberg were out of action for several months, and shipping on the Rhine was held up for a week. Damage from the 180-foot breach in the Eder reached Kassel, 35 miles away, with serious flooding of the streets and damage to several railway lines. Floodwater eventually extended more than 60 miles from the Eder.

The Germans compiled a dossier on 617 Squadron, calling them 'The Dam Raiders', 'The Dambusters' and 'Gibson's Boys'. All information apparently came from British newspapers such as *The Times*, *The Daily Telegraph*, *The Chronicle* and *The Manchester Guardian*. There was also a report from neutral Sweden: 'The flooding after the dams raid has created havoc. The town of Soest has for a long time been like an island and entire buildings were swept away. In Dortmund many streets were submerged and traffic restricted to flat bottom boats. The German soldiers of the 1914-18 war were saying that even the gunfire in Flanders had not been as destructive as the British attack on the Ruhr.' A State of Emergency was declared in Westphalia at 0400 on the morning of the raid: fifty miles below the Moehne at Meheim 130,000 people had been engulfed by the tidal wave in the early hours as coalfields and ironworks were swamped.

Left: The Eder with the huge breach on the left side. (U. Wolkers)

Below: An RAF reconnaissance photograph of the Eder dam after the raid, showing the breach. (IWM)

Right: Another view of the Eder. Waldeck Castle can just be seen in the upper right and it was from this direction that the attack came, hence the breach at lower left. (U. Wolkers)

Below right: Another view of the Eder looking directly towards Waldeck Castle. (U. Wolkers)

Above left: The railway line to Schwerte showing floodwater damage. (U. Wolkers)

Left: A lone German dispatch-rider wends his way through the flooded roads. (U. Wolkers)

Above: Hellparth Strasse near the Moehne dam. The water has reached the first-floor windows through which trapped people can be seen. (U. Wolkers)

Right: A view of the Moehne after the raid. (Karl Schutte)

Left: Work under way on the Moehne using conventional wooden scaffolding. Repairs were completed in only four months. (Karl Schutte)

Below left and centre: Repairs to the Eder. The primitive scaffolding makes it hard to understand why the target was not attacked again by conventional bombing. (U. Wolkers)

Below: The scale of the loss of water at the Moehne: the level is down to 58 million cubic metres instead of the usual 130 million. (Crown Copyright)

Casualties and Awards

British newspapers were naturally full of the raid; it captured the imagination of the public then and has continued to do so ever since. Headlines such as 'RAF Blow Up the Key Dams' and 'RAF Blow Up Three Dams in Germany' were commonplace. Harris was summoned to Buckingham Palace to receive the personal congratulations of the King while Wallis described the men of 617 as 'incomparable young men'. The leader of those men had the ribbon of the Victoria Cross sewn on his tunic — the announcement of the award had been made two days after 'Chastise'. Awards went to thirty-four members of the squadron: five DSOs, four bars to the DFC, ten DFCs, two CGMs, eleven DFMs and one bar to the DFM (unique in the history of 617). During the week following the raid the King and Queen visited the Squadron at Scampton and met aircrew and ground personnel of 617, as well as 57 Squadron who shared the same base. The raid was fully explained to them using the photographs and models of the dams, while a fully bombed-up Lancaster was on display, complete with bouncing bomb whose workings were explained by Barnes Wallis. The AOC of No 5 Group, Ralph Cochrane, and the station commander Scampton, Group Captain Charles Whitworth were also present.

On 21 June Gibson and the other men due for decoration left Lincoln for the investiture ceremony which was to take place the following day at Buckingham Palace at 10.15 a.m. For the first time since the reign of Queen Victoria the investiture was held by the Queen, King George being away inspecting warships in Algiers. The ceremony was also unusual in that Gibson was the first to be called forward; VCs were usually the last. Although on this occasion more than 300 awards were presented, the day belonged indisputably to The Dambusters; sadly, Sergeant John Pulford was ill and unable to receive his award in person. Gibson was now the highest decorated serving officer in the Royal Air Force, and was still only aged 24. The designer of the Lancaster bomber, Roy Chadwick, was also honoured with a CBE. Gibson said of the affair, 'I'm very glad to get that over with. The Queen was most charming and told me the King regretted not being there himself.'

In addition to the DSO, Flight Lieutenant McCarthy received the DFC for previous operations with 97 Squadron; Flight Sergeant Townsend, now a pilot officer, received the DFM for operations with 57 Squadron as well as the CGM; and Sergeant Franklin received the DFM for operations with 49 Squadron as well as a bar to the DFM for the Dams operation. It was a happy party that attended the dinner arranged by A.V. Roe, the manufacturers of the Lancaster, at a restaurant in Lower Regent Street. The menus were inscribed 'The Dambusters' and the name was first officially mooted. Barnes Wallis received a large photograph of the Moehne Dam with the signature of Gibson in the breach. Gibson was given a silver model of a Lancaster. Typically he was unwilling to be the centre of attention and his words of tribute remain valid fifty years on: 'The success of the attack on the dams was due to hundreds of technicians and above all to the AOC of the Group and the Senior Staff Officer. We flying crews are indebted to them.'

Inevitably their had been losses: of the nineteen Lancasters that took off eight failed to return. Of the fifty-six men missing, all but three were reported killed, three were taken prisoner. Twenty-seven of the dead are buried in the Reichswald War Cemetery, five in the Rhineberg War Cemetery, seven in the Bergen Op Zoom War Cemetery, seven in the Bergen General Cemetery and one in the Harlington War Cemetery. The remaining six have no known grave and are remembered on the Runnymede Memorial. Barnes Wallis refused to accept credit for the success of the Dambusters who continued to use his special weapons throughout the war. When asked about the losses they suffered he was unequivocal: 'Miserable, utterly wretched. If I had known I would never had started the idea.' An interesting postscript to the story came in 1981 when the Hessen Scout Troop created a memorial to peace on the spot where Pilot Officer Ottley's Lancaster crashed in Kohlinggen Forest. The only surviving member of his crew, Freddie Tees, who was taken prisoner on the Dams raid, placed a wreath at the unveiling in memory of his fallen comrades.

Left: Wing Commander Guy Gibson at the head of his men during the Royal visit to Scampton on 26 May 1943. On his right, Squadron Leader Maltby and left, Flight Lieutenant Martin. (IWM)

Below: Wing Commander Gibson and four of his crew. (IWM)

Right: Flight Lieutenant Les Munro being presented to the King at Scampton in 1943. Left to right: Munro, Cochrane, HM King George VI, Gibson. (British Aerospace)

Below right: Les Munro signing autographs at the 40th anniversary of 'Chastise' outside Lincoln Cathedral in May 1983. He is now a sheep farmer in New Zealand. (Author)

Above left: Flight Lieutenant Shannon being presented to the King at Scampton. Left to right: Shannon, Group Captain Whitworth, Cochrane, HM The King, Gibson. (IWM)

Left: David Shannon, now a retired businessman and living in London, signs autographs outside Lincoln Cathedral in May 1983. (Author)

Above: Ken Brown, awarded the CGM for his attack on the Sorpe in May 1943, leaving Lincoln Cathedral after the 40th anniversary service. (Author)

Right: Flight Lieutenant Joe McCarthy being presented to the Queen in May 1943. He was awarded the DSO for his attack on the Sorpe. (IWM)

Above right: Joe McCarthy at the Petwood Hotel for the 40th anniversary in 1983. (Bill Howarth)

Above: Flight Lieutenant Micky Martin being presented to HM The King at Scampton in May 1943. Left to right: Martin, Whitworth, HM The King, Gibson, Cochrane. (IWM)

Above right: Micky Martin, now Air Marshal Sir Harold Martin (retd), with Dame Vera Lynn at the Bomber Command Association dinner in 1980. He was president of the Association at the time. (Derek Warren)

Right: Wing Commander Guy and Eve Gibson at Buckingham Palace for the investiture of his Victoria Cross in June 1943. (Author)

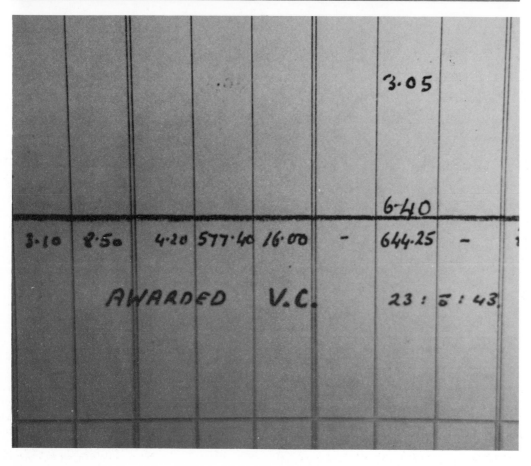

Left: The entry made by Gibson in his log-book after 'Chastise'. (Author)

Right: Gibson and Roy Chadwick, designer of the Lancaster bomber, at Buckingham Palace where they received the VC and CBE respectively. Behind Gibson is newly commissioned Pilot Officer Ken Brown who had just been awarded the CGM, the highest award for a non-commissioned officer in the RAF. (Mrs. Dove)

Left: The entry in Gibson's log-book on 23 May 1943, noting that he had been awarded the VC. (Author)

Right: Wing Commander Gibson and Squadron Leader Maltby in Gibson's office at No 2 Hangar RAF Scampton. This wartime photograph was unusual in that it was in full colour. (IWM)

Above: *Gibson's decorations: VC, DSO and bar, DFC and bar. (IWM)*

Left: *Gibson signs a large photograph of the breached Moehne dam which was later presented to Barnes Wallis. (MOD copyright)*

44

Above: Guy Gibson is presented with a silver model Lancaster by the directors of A.V. Roe as Charles Whitworth, the station commander at Scampton, looks on. (MOD copyright)

Right: Barnes Wallis inspects his Moehne dam photograph. (B. Wallis)

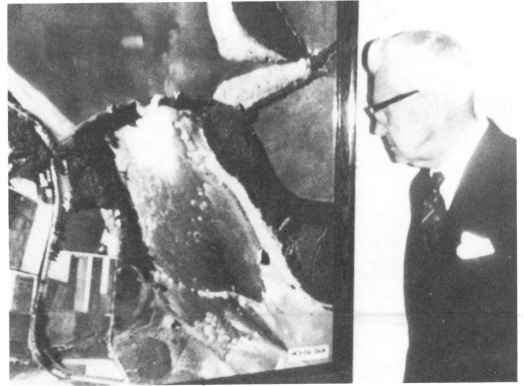

Left: Gibson is toasted by his fellow dambusters at the celebration dinner in June 1943. Left to right: unknown, Trevor-Roper, Spafford, Sumpter, Maltby, unknown, Caple. (MOD copyright)

Below Left: Gibson reaffirms his Scout promise with 1st Tovil Troop at Maidstone in 1943. (G. Coombe)

Right: Flight Lieutenant Hopgood's crashed aircraft being inspected by the Germans the day after the raid. (Karl Schutte)

Below: Flight Lieutenant Barlow's crashed aircraft after the raid. One of the propellers is visible in the lower right-hand corner, and the tail wheel is still attached to a large part of the tail. (N. Kruger)

Left: *The Oxford/Cambridge boat race of 2 April 1938. No 2 in the Oxford crew was Henry Young, flight commander of 617 Squadron, who was killed on the dams raid. (The Times)*

Below Left: *Squadron Leader 'Dinghy' Young's crashed aircraft. Only Young and another crew member survived; the fate of the others has never been determined. (G. Zwanenberg)*

Below: *The sole survivor of Pilot Officer Ottley's crew was Flight Sergeant Freddie Tees, seen here revisiting the site of his crash in Germany. (F. Tees)*

49

Reference :-
DD/6/43

No. 617 Squadron, RAF Station,
Scampton, Lincs.

20th. May, 1943.

My Dear Mrs Tees,

It is with deep regret that I write to confirm my telegram advising you that your son, Sergeant F. Tees, is missing as a result of operations on the night of May 16/17th., 1943.

Your son was Front Gunner of an aircraft detailed to carry out an attack against the Mohne Dam. Contact with this aircraft was lost after it took off, and nothing further was heard from it.

It is possible that the crew were able to abandon the aircraft and land safely in enemy territory, in which case news will reach you direct from the International Red Cross Committee within the next six weeks. The captain of your son's aircraft, Pilot Officer Ottley, was an experienced and able pilot, and would, I am sure, do everything possible to ensure the safety of his crew.

Please accept my sincere sympathy during this anxious period of waiting.

I have arranged for your son's personal effects to be taken care of by the Committee of Adjustment Officer at this Station, and these will be forwarded to you through normal channels in due course.

If there is any way in which I can help you, please let me know.

Yours Very Sincerely,

G.P. Gibson
Wing Commander,
Commanding, 617 Squadron, RAF.

Mrs. E. Tees,
23, St. James Rd.,
Chichester, Sussex.

Left: The letter that Freddie Tees' mother received on 20 May 1943 informing her that her son was missing from operations. (F. Tees)

Left: Waldeck Castle after the attack on the Eder. The castle was used as a landmark by the navigators. Today it is a restaurant. (U. Wolkers)

Post-Dams

Remarkably, in view of the success of the raid, there was some thought given to disbanding 617 and returning the experienced crews to their original squadrons, or transferring them to training units as instructors. This idea was quickly abandoned and the Squadron was retained for low-level attacks against special targets. Two new crews were drafted in and Wing Commander Holden DSO, DFC took over from Gibson. Under Holden, the Squadron flew their first mission — an electrical power plant at Acqua Sciva north of Milan on 15 July. Poor visibility over the target meant blind bombing with unsatisfactory results; conditions over another target at San Polo D'Enza were similarly unsuitable, so 617's first missions after their great start were disappointing. They returned to Italy on the 24th to bomb Leghorn and on the 29th to drop leaflets.

August 1943 saw the Squadron move from Scampton to Coningsby, also in Lincolnshire, and the home of 619 Squadron. On 14 September an attack on the Dortmund–Ems Canal was aborted, and on turning for home across the North Sea Squadron Leader Maltby's aircraft hit the water and he and his crew were killed. A second operation next day was equally costly with flak accounting for Wing Commander Holden and Flight Lieutenant Knight who crashed on the return trip after hitting tree-tops. Two other aircrew also failed to return. The Squadron next attacked the viaduct at Antheor near Cannes in the South of France. More than 540 feet long and 185 high, it was estimated that at least 14,000 tons of military supplies passed over the viaduct each day en route to the German troops in Italy. The Squadron attacked the viaduct repeatedly but failed to destroy it.

In November 1943 the arrival of the highly experienced Wing Commander Leonard Cheshire to command the Squadron coincided with a change of targets for 617. After months of operations against special targets, they were now called upon to attack the sites in northern France and Holland from which Flying Bombs were being launched daily against London and southern England. These sites were usually concealed in woodland, but the conspicuous concrete launching ramps made them relatively easy to identify from the air. Cheshire insisted that 617 do all their own target marking rather than depend on other squadrons, and this became another area in which the Squadron excelled.

In January 1944 the Dambusters moved to Woodhall Spa where they remained for the rest of the war. Here they were joined by an American, Lieutenant Knilans, who had joined the RCAF pre-1941 before transferring to the USAAF. Curiously, he never flew with his fellow countrymen, but he completed forty operations with 617 Squadron.

Above left: Gibson meets Mrs Taerum, the mother of one of his crew members, during his visit to Canada in August 1943. Taerum was killed on operations a few weeks later. (M. M. Taerum)

Left: A 617 Squadron Lancaster taxiing at Blida airfield in North Africa in July 1943. (Bill Howarth)

Above left: Flight Lieutenant Les Knight was awarded the DSO for his attack on the Eder dam in May 1943. He was later to die while trying to crash-land his aircraft in Holland after allowing his crew to bail out. (H. Hobday)

Above: Hoby Hobday visiting his pilot's grave while on the run from the Germans. He later managed to get back to England. (H. Hobday)

Left: The Antheor viaduct in 1943. (Author)

Below: The Petwood Hotel which was used as the 617 Squadron officers' mess. (Author)

Right: *The wartime layout of the Petwood Hotel. (Author)*

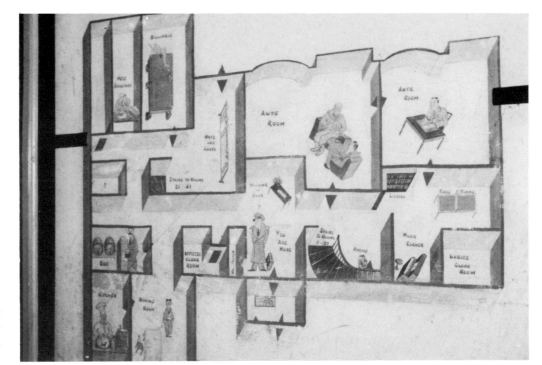

Below right: *Lieutenant Nick Knilans, USAAF. He never flew with his compatriots, but he did fly 40 operations with 617 and a number previously with 619. He was awarded the DSO and DFC. (N. Knilans)*

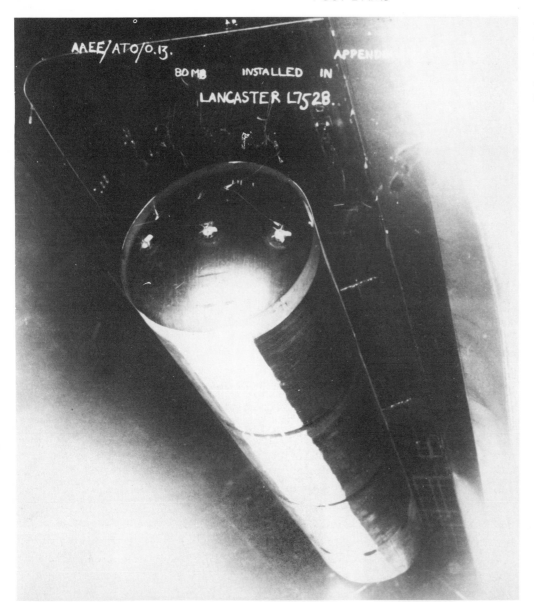

Left: A 12,000-pound blockbuster as used by 617 Squadron before they received Tallboy. Using this they became known as the Factory Busters. (Crown Copyright)

Left: A Tallboy on display outside the Battle of Britain Memorial Flight's home at Coningsby. The author standing next to it shows the size of the bomb. (Author)

'Tallboy'

Barnes Wallis continued to feature in the history of 617 and in early 1944 he produced another secret weapon which he felt would help shorten the war. Five years earlier he had been working on a paper (published 1940) entitled 'A Method of Attacking the Axis Powers'. In this he had outlined a plan for a 10-ton bomb which, if dropped from a great altitude, would create an earthquake effect around a target and literally shake it to pieces. Now, a smaller, 6-ton bomb with similar but lesser effects was produced and christened 'Tallboy'.

Until now the RAF's heaviest bomb had been the 4,000-pound 'Cookie' which was essentially a blast type device. With it 617 devastated almost one-third of the factories in the French industrial town of Clermont Ferrand in March 1944, and the Squadron almost became known as 'The Factory Busters'. After a raid against a powder factory on 18 March Cheshire signalled: 'The powder works would appear to have outlived its usefulness.'

Attacking an aircraft production factory at Lyons on 25 March, as part of the Allied campaign to cripple the Luftwaffe, Cheshire used four Mosquito aircraft to mark the target and attacked from low level with 100 per cent incendiaries. But even experts could make mistakes and the raid failed to inflict any serious damage on the plant.

Wallis meanwhile was perfecting Tallboy. Twenty-one feet of shining blue-back steel weighing more than 12,000 pounds, its production had required the efforts of 22,000 Sheffield steel workers. Precision-built, the aero-dynamic tail fin caused the bomb to spin faster and hence achieve pin-point accuracy. On one of the first trial drops an unarmed Tallboy buried itself ninety feet into the Ashley Walk bombing range in the New Forest, and when filled with the explosive RDX the resulting crater was eighty feet deep and one hundred feet in diameter.

617 Squadron received their first weapons in late May and did not have long to wait before using them. On 8 June 1944 they flew a mission against the Saumur railway tunnel in the Loire valley. Destruction of the tunnel would block the flow of reinforcements to the German forces in Normandy and greatly assist the Allied invasion. Each Tallboy was filled with 5,000 pounds of RDX set with a time fuze of 25 seconds, the time it would take to fall and bury itself in the tunnel before exploding upwards. Twenty Lancasters and three Mosquitos took part, together with ten Lancasters from 83 Squadron to act as flare markers.

Several direct hits on the tunnel were observed. One struck close to the southern entrance; two more destroyed hundreds of feet of the permanent way. The Tallboy that penetrated the roof of the tunnel caused a colossal landslide within the tunnel, more than 10,000 tons of earth collapsing into the crater. The vital line was never used again.

Further Tallboy missions were flown against the pens at Le Havre where numerous E-boats were based. Twenty-one Lancasters led by Squadron Leader Munro bombed the target marked by Wing Commander Cheshire and post-raid reconnaissance showed that most craft were destroyed by a huge tidal wave created by the exploding bombs, and the pens were heavily damaged. Attacks against the V-1 and V-2 rocket sites continued and on 24 June the site at Wizernes was attacked for the third time. Two Lancasters were shot down, but again the Tallboy did tremendous damage. Thirty-eight years later a survivor from one of the Lancasters, Gerry Hobbs, returned to Wizernes and was given his parachute harness by a local Frenchman who had helped in his rescue.

In July 1944 Cheshire completed his 100th operation, received the VC and third bar to his DSO and was taken off operational flying together with Shannon, Munro and McCarthy. Command of the Squadron was taken by Wing Commander Willie Tait who had more than 100 ops in his log-book, two DSOs and a DFC. Later that month the V-weapons storage facility in a limestone cave at Rilly la Montagne near Rheims was nominated for 617's attention. The operation called for 617 to bomb from 12,000 feet — well below the main force above them. Any stray or late bombing and 617 would be in trouble. Protests were made but ignored and sure enough one Lancaster was hit by falling bombs; the aircraft flown by Flight Lieutenant Bill Reid, VC, suffered damage to fuselage, rudders and elevators and spun into the ground, only Reid and another crew member surviving.

The Squadron soon reverted to attacking the U-boat pens for which Tallboy had originally been intended. Conventional bombing had merely chipped the massive ferro-concrete pens, but with Tallboys the Dambusters destroyed the complexes at Brest, Lorient, La Pallice and Ijmuiden. The target lists continued to include bridges such as the one in August at Etaples in August: a vital link for the German forces moving south-west from Courtrai and for the route to Belgium. This was the only operation in which a squadron other than 617 dropped Tallboy and although the bridge was hit by both 617 and No 9 Squadrons it was not brought down. In fact 9 Squadron would team up with 617 again for they both had a prize target in the offing.

Left: *A Tallboy being prepared for delivery to the Squadron. (IWM)*

Right: The difficult task of getting the Tallboy into the bomb-bay of the Lancaster. Note the strong leather strapping to hold the bomb securely. (Frank Hawkins)

Right: A Lancaster armed with a Tallboy warming up for take-off. (IWM)

Above: Ashley Walk bombing
range in Hampshire, where
Tallboy and Grand Slam bombs
were tested. (H. Wills)

Left: The Saumur tunnel in
France was attacked in June
1944 and remained blocked until
after the war. (Crown Copyright)

Above: The Saumur tunnel today. The difficulty of accurately bombing such a small target can be imagined. (N. Knilans)

Right: A well-cratered Saumur Tunnel. (IWM)

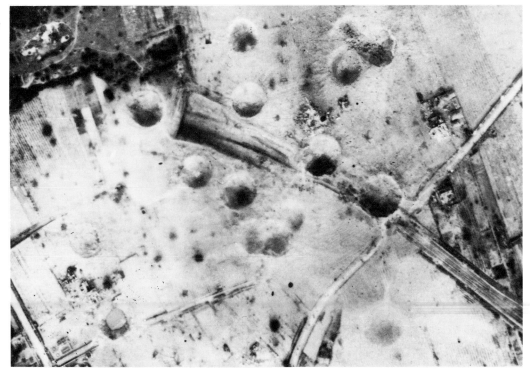

Above: The E-boat pens at Le Havre. One roof has been brought down completely by a Tallboy hit. (IWM)

Left: Flight Lieutenant Les Munro and his navigator Len Chalmers who both took part in the dams raid in 1943. (IWM)

Right: The Wizernes rocket site before 617 Squadron's attack in 1944. (IWM)

Below: The rocket site on 4 November 1944 after the attack, showing a typical Tallboy crater. (IWM)

Above: The Wizernes rocket site revisited in 1980 by Gerry Hobbs, who was shot down while attacking it. Hobbs is on the right; to the left is Andr Schamp, a Frenchman who helped Hobbs after his landing. (L'Ind pendant)

Left: Hobbs recovering the parachute that he last saw in 1944. André Schamp had kept it for more than forty years in the hope that one day its owner would return. (L'Indépendant)

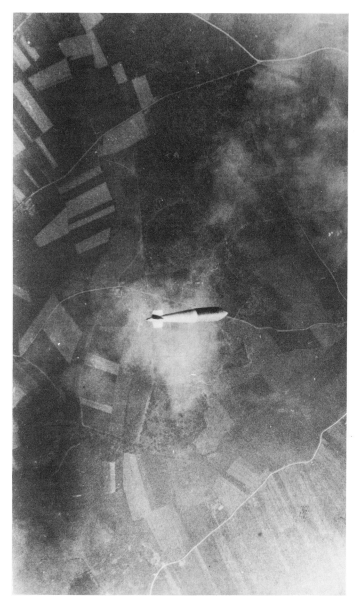

Above: A Tallboy photographed on its way to the Watten rocket site in northern France on 19 June 1944. The bomb was dropped from 16,000 feet; the site was completely destroyed. (Crown Copyright)

Above right: Flying Officer Nick Ross at the Petwood Hotel. He managed to drop his bomb manually during the Watten attack after the release mechanism had failed. (N. Ross)

Right: Nick Knilans standing beside a Tallboy at the RAF Museum Hendon. (Author)

Left: *The German battleship Tirpitz in Alta Fiord, Norway in 1944. After locating and attacking her here in September, 617 crippled the ship and forced her relocation to Tromso. (Crown Copyright)*

Tirpitz

The 45,000-ton German battleship *Tirpitz* was one of the largest capital ships in western waters, with a main armament of eight 15-inch, twelve 5.9-inch and sixteen 4.1-inch guns plus a host of smaller anti-aircraft weapons. With an armoured deck five inches thick and up to fifteen inches of armour on her sides, she was a formidable target.

617 first became involved with *Tirpitz* in September 1944 when armed with the Tallboy bombs that had already been used to good effect on other difficult targets. The distance to Alta Fiord was too great for the Lancasters to be able to return to base without refuelling so 617 and 9 Squadrons flew on to Russian territory at Yagodnik after hitting *Tirpitz* with one Tallboy. Terrible weather and navigational problems forced many aircraft to land wherever they could before fuel ran out. Flying Officer Ian Ross was down to his last 30 gallons before finding a suitable landing strip. Even then Russian troops obstructed the runway which forced him to crash-land at Molotoush. Another casualty was Squadron Leader Wyness whose brakes failed to stop his Lancaster which slid off the runway and sustained damage to the port undercarriage. On the return flight Flying Officer Levy's Lancaster crashed into mountains at Rukkedalen and he and his crew are buried there.

But the main target remained afloat. On 16 October *Tirpitz* was moved to Haakoy Island near Tromso with the intention of using her as a floating fortress. Significantly, however, she was now 200 miles closer to UK airbases and now 617 could attack and return to base: a round trip of 2,252 miles. Some modifications were needed to squeeze this range from the Lancaster: Merlin 24 engines and new propellers were installed, and the mid-upper turret was removed to allow extra fuel tanks to be installed; pilots' armour plating was removed and the rear-turret carried 3,000 fewer rounds of .303-inch ammunition.

Taking off from Lossiemouth on 29 October, each aircraft carried 2,406 gallons of fuel and the crew was reduced to six for the 13-hour flight. Climbing initially to 4,000 feet then through 8,000 to bombing height of 15,000 feet, the force cruised at 160 to 180 miles per hour. Over Haakoy, however, cloud allowed only brief glimpses of the target and the bombing was inaccurate. Only one Tallboy fell near the ship, but according to the German Navy Operations Staff's War Diary *Tirpitz* was too badly damaged to move again. One Lancaster was shot down and crash-landed at Porjus, in Sweden, where the remains exist to this day.

A third and it was to be hoped final mission was planned for November but there were only five suitable days forecast for a successful raid. After that the Arctic winter would prevent attacks until the spring of 1945. A planned raid on 5 November was cancelled, but 617 and 9 Squadrons flew to Lossiemouth on 11 November. There was some talk of each aircraft carrying six smaller bombs in the hope that some might hit the ship, but the known effects of a Tallboy explosion close to the warship's hull won the argument and at 0259 on 12 November the first aircraft — NG181 — took off followed by seventeen others.

As they made their rendezvous over Akka Lake the squadrons' aircraft were spotted by lookouts at 0805 and a protective smoke-screen was laid over the fiord. This time the Lancasters were too quick for the defences and Wing Commander Tait bombed a clear target at 0841, probably striking *Tirpitz* near her athwartships catapult. Further strikes were recorded just off the bows, the port side, the starboard quarter and near the ship's funnel; after the eighth observed explosion the ship was seen to heel to starboard. From waves and disturbance observed near the stern, it was thought that the force of repeated explosions following one another so quickly in such a confined area physically lifted the battleship out of the water by approximately twelve feet. The ninth bomb burst abreast of 'Y' turret and immediately a high column of thick smoke erupted from the ship, followed by a flash from amidships. The final bomb fell at 0851 and defensive gunfire had by then all but ceased.

German records reveal that the first bomb hit forward and destroyed all electrical services. One near miss made a dent in the hull sixty feet long and began the roll-over, followed twenty minutes into the attack by a huge explosion which blew a 120-foot hole in the keel. Observers aboard the PRU Lancaster from 463 Squadron saw *Tirpitz* heel to 80 degrees, showing her red keel, and continue to roll until her superstructure hit the lake bed.

The Secretary of State for Air, Sir Archibald Sinclair, visited Woodhall personally to congratulate the squadrons on their good job. In September 1945 the great battleship still lay rusting, with more than 1,000 of her crew entombed. By 1950 there was virtually nothing left following the attentions of a salvage firm from Oslo.

Left: Flying Officer Ian Ross crash-landed his Lancaster in Russia. On examination it was found that only 30 gallons of fuel remained in the tanks. (Crown Copyright)

Below: Flying Officer Carey's aircraft NF 920-E-Easy still lying in Sweden, 48 years after it crashed. (Hanssen)

Right: NF 920 still bears the word 'Easy' on it's fuselage. (Hanssen)

Right: Flying Officer Sanders and his crew next to their Tirpitz-bound Lancaster ME 562-K. Sanders is third right. (IWM)

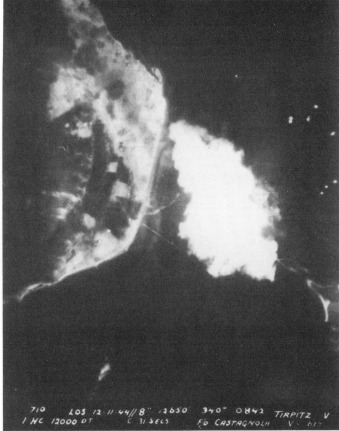

1982 W.S. 12.11.44// 8" 13000 340° 0841   TIRPITZ D
1 HC 12000 DT.   C 31 SECS   W/C TAIT. D 617

710   LOS 12.11.44// 8" 12650   340" 0842   TIRPITZ V
1 HC 12000 DT.   C 31 SECS   F/O CASTAGNOLA V · 617

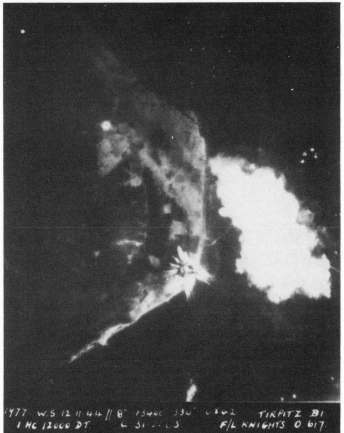

LOS 12.11.44/ 8 3200 340° 0842   TIRPITZ A
1 HC 12000 DT.   C 31 SEC   F/O GINGLES A 617

1477 W.S. 12.11.44// 8" 13400 330" 0842   TIRPITZ B1
1 HC 12000 DT.   C 31 SECS   F/L KNIGHTS O 617

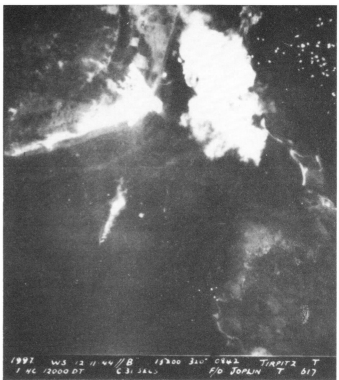

Opposite page, top left: Wing Commander Tait's bombing photo of Tirpitz on 12 November 1944. Bomb dropped at 0841 from 13,000 feet. (PRO)

Opposite page, top right: Flying Officer Castagnola's bombing photo: 0842 at 12,650 feet. (PRO)

Opposite page, bottom left: Flying Officer Gingle's bombing photo: 0842 at 13,200 feet. (PRO)

Opposite page, bottom right: Flight Lieutenant Knight's bombing photo: 0842 at 13,400 feet. (PRO)

Above left: Flying Officer Lee's bombing photo: 0842 at 14,400 feet. (PRO)

Above: Flying Officer Joplin's bombing photo: 0842 at 15,200 feet. (PRO)

Below left: Flying Officer Watts' bombing photo: 0843 at 13,800 feet. (PRO)

Below: Flight Lieutenant Dobson's bombing photo: 0843 at 15,800 feet. (PRO)

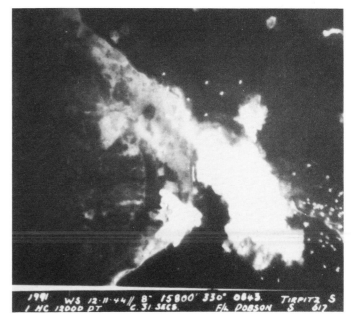

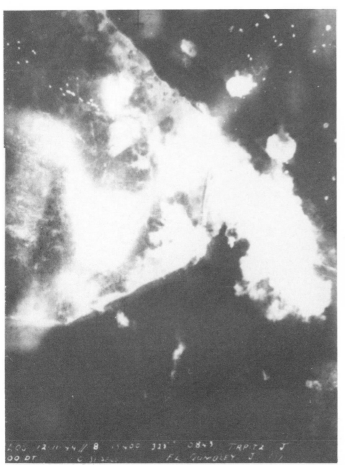

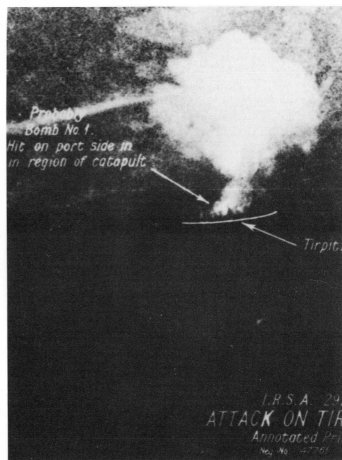

Probably
Bomb No 1.
Hit on port side in
in region of catapult

Tirpitz

I.R.S.A. 29
ATTACK ON TIR
Annotated Pri
Neg No 47761

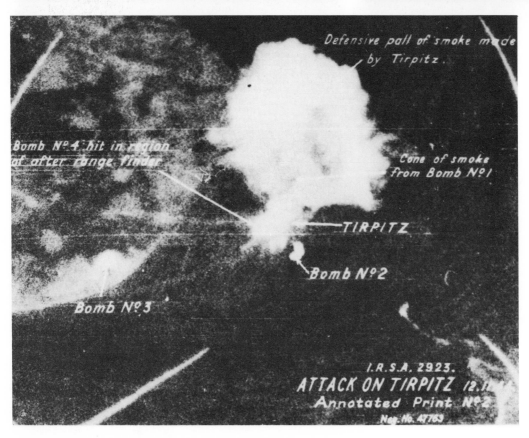

Defensive pall of smoke made
by Tirpitz.

Bomb Nº 4 hit in region
of after range finder

Cone of smoke
from Bomb Nº 1

TIRPITZ

Bomb Nº 2

Bomb Nº 3

I.R.S.A. 2923.
ATTACK ON TIRPITZ 12.1
Annotated Print Nº 2
Neg No 47763

Above left: Flight Lieutenant Gumbley's bombing photo: 0843 at 15,400 feet. (PRO)

Above: The beginning of the attack on Tirpitz showing the first bomb dropped by Tait scoring a direct hit. (PRO)

Left: The attack develops with hits by Nos 2 and 3 bombs. (PRO)

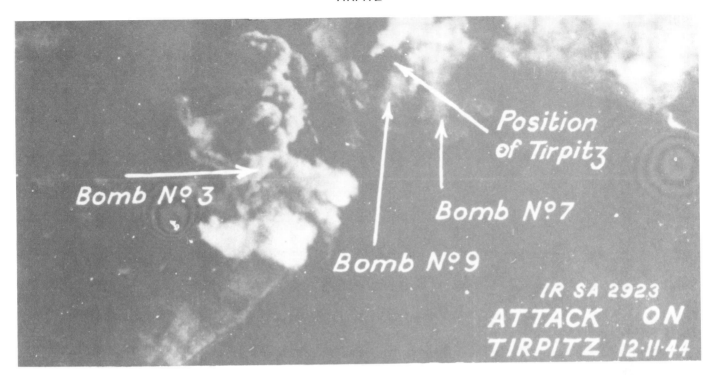

Bomb Nº 3

Position of Tirpitz

Bomb Nº 7

Bomb Nº 9

IR SA 2923
ATTACK ON
TIRPITZ 12·11·44

Above: *Bombs Nos 7 and 9 hitting the ship. (PRO)*

Right: *Newspaper coverage of the sinking of Tirpitz on 12 November 1944.*

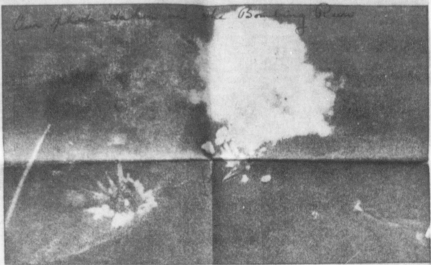

RAF SINK TIRPITZ

At 10.30 a.m. Tirpitz was hit and a few seconds later this picture was taken as smoke billowed out from the bombs. She was still visible, but by 10.45 she was on fire, and as the last aircraft turned for home she keeled over.

'QUAKE' BOMBS DO IT
Down She Went in Few Minutes

BOMBER COMMAND Lancasters have sunk the Tirpitz with 12,000lb. earthquake bombs. She is lying upside down in Tromso Fiord with her keel above water.

The R.A.F. tried twice before to sink Hitler's last big battleship—she was 45,000 tons and sister ship of the Bismarck—but they could not see her properly for smokescreens and low cloud.

In this last raid the weather was perfect, there were no smokescreens. One 12,000-pounder hit her amidships, another in the bows, a third towards the stern, and there were two "very near misses" which must have done extensive underwater damage.

The attack began at 10.30 a.m.—at 10.45 she was heeling over rapidly.

They Saw Her Go

The last air crew to leave saw her go. The rear-gunner of the machine, an R.A.A.F. aircraft sent to film the attack, describing her

✦ Facts About ✦
The Tirpitz

TIRPITZ was an "April Fool" launched in Hitler's presence on April 1, 1939. She was laid down in 1936 and completed in 1941.

She was never in action against Allied ships. She raided Spitzbergen once, but that was her only operational sortie.

First spotted in Norwegian waters in January 1942, she had been hounded ever since by the Navy and R.A.F.

She was 759 feet long, had a

Wing-Comdr. J. B. Tait, D.S.O., D.F.C.

Top left: *Tirpitz, capsized after the attack in Tromso Fiord. (Author)*

Bottom left: *The keel of the sunken battleship. (Author)*

Above: *A view of Tirpitz taken from Haakoy Island. (Lars Thorsen)*

Below: *Tirpitz seen from Tromso. (Lars Thorsen)*

Left: *The upturned battleship is examined by German sailors soon after she capsized. Above them is the huge propeller shaft. (IWM)*

Right: *Work on the starboard propeller shaft. (Einar Hovding)*

Right: *A workman standing next to 32cm armour plate. (Einar Hovding)*

Far right: *A 200-ton bow section being raised. (Einar Hovding)*

Left: *Each main 38cm gun weighed 138 tons. (Einar Hovding)*

Right: *The 110cm-thick armoured deck. (Einar Hovding)*

Left: *Lifting a 10.5cm gun. (Einar Hovding)*

Right: *View of salvage operations from starboard. (Einar Hovding)*

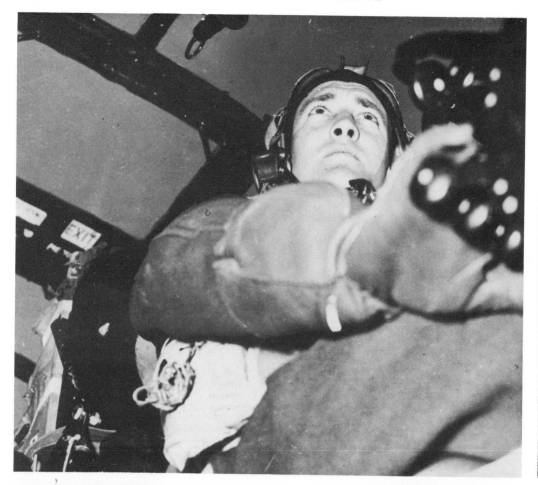

Above left: *Flight Lieutenant Bruce Buckham flew a 46523 Squadron Lancaster from Waddington to film the attack and the sinking of Tirpitz. This historic film can now be seen at the Imperial War Museum. (IWM)*

Left: *Flight Lieutenant Levy and his crew, buried where they crashed on the way back from Russia after the first Tirpitz attack in Alta Fiord. (E. E. S. Peck)*

Above: *The magnificent Tirpitz, 'Queen of the North'. (Author)*

Right: *The Secretary of State for Air, Sir Archibald Sinclair, arriving at the Petwood Hotel to congratulate 617 Squadron on their success. (Author)*

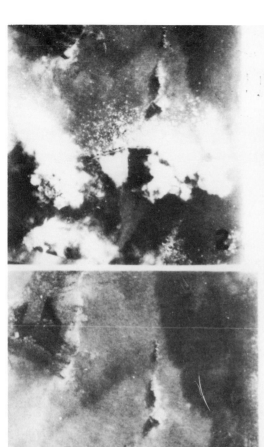

133. THE URFT DAM. December 8th 1944
1. Dam at 11.10hrs.
2. Early in attack showing bomb
   bursts around the target.
3. (a) The Spillway at 11.12 hrs.
   (b) Position of Dam under smo'...

Above: The attack on the Urft dam on 8 December 1944. Note the bomb bursts around the target. (Crown Copyright)

Left: Squadron Leader Tony Iveson's aircraft NG 181-M after its return from Bergen on 12 January 1945. The damage was inflicted by Fw 190 fighters and flak in the target area. The tail fin on the port side was blasted away, but despite this and the loss of one engine Iveson brought the aircraft home to the Shetlands. (A. Iveson)

'Grand Slam'

The Squadron was soon back in action with another operation at the army's request: an attack against the Urft dam at the head of the Roer valley. Below the dam American forces were preparing to cross the river but wanted the dam destroyed in order to weaken enemy resistance. Although the raid damaged the top of the dam the Germans were able to reduce the water level and minimize the damage. Called into action on 12 January 1945 against the U-boat pens and ships at Bergen in Norway, 617 and 9 Squadrons flew with fighter escort which was certainly required when Luftwaffe fighters met the bombers. Squadron Leader Iveson's aircraft was seriously damaged and three of his crew baled out, but Iveson was able to fly the aircraft back to base. He was awarded the DFC. Flying Officer Ross was attacked and forced to ditch off the coast of Norway, but sadly he and his crew in their dinghy were machine-gunned and killed by German fighters.

The Bielefeld viaduct was again attacked in February and despite greatly increased defences two sections of the viaduct were destroyed over a distance of 135 feet. By now Barnes Wallis had perfected a much greater version of Tallboy — the 22,000-pound 'Grand Slam'. Carrying new squadron letters of 'YZ' each Lancaster had bomb bay modifications and strengthened undercarriage. Known as BI Specials, they flew without wireless operators or mid-upper gunners. Thus equipped 617 took off on 14 March 1945, led by Squadron Leader Calder, and bombed from about 12,000 feet on a clear target. The effects were devastating with huge sections of the viaduct literally shaken to pieces. Grand Slam was again used against the Arnsberg viaduct with another success on 19 March, and against U-boat pens at Farge, Bremen, where considerable damage was done on the 27th to these previously impregnable bunkers. For 617 Squadron the war ended on 25 April when they formed part of a force numbering 350 aircraft to bomb Berchtesgaden, Hitler's alpine retreat, which was left in ruins.

More than 95 targets had been attacked by 617 in just over two years, and although other squadron crews were operating every night, most 617 personnel had already completed one tour of operations and were now flying against heavily defended targets. The role of 617 was special in that their missions required the highest levels of flying skill and dedication in attacking vital targets that deprived the enemy of much-needed resources. The value of such operations is not easy to assess and one can only speculate as to the effects on the war if the targets had not been attacked and destroyed. The historian has therefore to balance his conclusions against an overall perspective of how wars are fought: the one criteria paramount at all times is that of attacking the enemy wherever possible and denying him his resources of war. The efforts of 617 Squadron in this direction were of the highest order and of major importance in winning the Second World War.

Above: *Flying Officer Ian Ross and his crew, sadly lost on the Bergen operation after being attacked by fighters and ditching. Having got into the dinghy they were promptly shot up in the water, only one body ever being found.*

Below left and right: *The Bielefeld viaduct after the attack in 1945. (Crown Copyright)*

Above: The viaduct in 1947. This photograph was taken by Flight Lieutenant Len Sumpter who took part in 617's first operation — the dams raid — and in their last operation, in 1945. (L. Sumpter)

Below: The biggest bomb of the war, the Grand Slam, seen leaving a Lancaster bomber. (Crown Copyright)

Below: The crater left by Grand Slam bomb trials, possibly at Ashley Walk bombing range in 1945. (IWM)

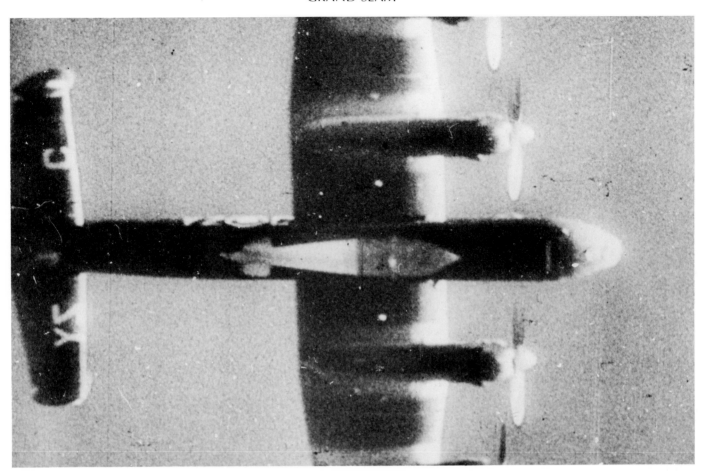

Top Left: A view of Grand Slam as strapped under a Lancaster before an attack on 19 March 1945. Note the 'YZ' on the tailplane denoting that it was a Grand Slam carrying aircraft. (IWM)

Left: A painting of Squadron Leader Jock Calder, the first of 617's pilots to drop the Grand Slam bomb. (Maurice Gardner)

Above: The operation against the U-boat construction works at Farge in Germany. Some 800 tons of concrete was brought down per crater. (IWM)

Left: *The attack on the Arbergen railway bridge in Germany on 21 March 1945. Squadron Leader Cockshott's (aircraft, letter 'B') bomb fell very near the bridge; the blast from Grand Slam was usually sufficient to topple most such structures. (IWM)*

Right: *The accuracy of Martin's bomb-aimer. (IWM)*

Right: *Two shots of the Arnsberg viaduct taken after the operation, showing the damage Grand Slam caused. (Crown Copyright)*

Left: *The attack on Arnsberg on 19 March 1945 was a great success, and Flight Lieutenant Phil Martin flying PG 996-C scored a direct hit on the viaduct, cutting two spans completely. The film of this can be seen at the Imperial War Museum. Martin is seen here before the attack.*

Left: The attack on the midget submarine pens at Poortershaven, Holland in February 1945. (Crown Copyright)

Right: The last target for 617 Squadron during the Second World War: the Eagle's Lair, Hitler's HQ at Berchtesgaden in April 1945. (IWM)

Right: Barnes Wallis flying with a 617 Squadron crew in 1945. (617 Squadron, Marham)

Top left: *A group photograph of 'B' Flight, 617 Squadron in 1945. (Author)*

Bottom left: *Flying Officer Castagnola and his crew in 1945. Left to right: Gorringe, Ronald, Eaves, Castagnola, Henderson, Evans, unknown. (Author)*

Above: *617 Squadron groundcrew in front of a 617 Mosquito at Woodhall Spa in 1944. (Author)*

Below: *The Moehne as seen in 1945 by the advancing Allied troops. (IWM)*

Left and above: Barnes Wallis with an unknown member of 617 Squadron visiting the Moehne dam in April 1945. (Crown Copyright)

Below left and right: Wallis visits the Arnsberg viaduct in 1945 and finds the nose of one of his Grand Slam bombs. The spot where he found it is arrowed. (Crown Copyright)

Post-War

In May 1945 Operation 'Exodus' began, its aim being to get all Allied prisoners of war back home as soon as possible. On VE Day, 8 May, 617 flew their first mission to Brussels via Juvincourt and continued to bring back ex-prisoners until 15 May. During this period the whole of No 5 Group flew 909 sorties and returned 18,133 POWs, while from April to June Bomber Command brought home almost 80,000 Allied servicemen, and earned the personal congratulations of the Allied Supreme Commander, Dwight Eisenhower. There followed further non-operational flights known as 'Cooks Tours' as the bomber crews took the men and women of their ground personnel to see the targets they had flown against.

Barnes Wallis did some visiting of his own during the immediate post-war months, with visits to the Moehne Dam and the Arnsberg viaduct: at the former he found all torpedo netting still in place, at the latter he discovered an intact nose cone from one of his Grand Slam bombs. 617 were now far from their old targets, having been transferred to Digri in India in January 1946 to help quell the Indian naval mutiny in Bombay. Happily they were not needed and before returning to RAF Binbrook in late 1946 they took part in the Delhi Air Show.

Right: 617 Squadron Lancasters fly over Delhi during the Delhi Air Show in 1946. (Author)

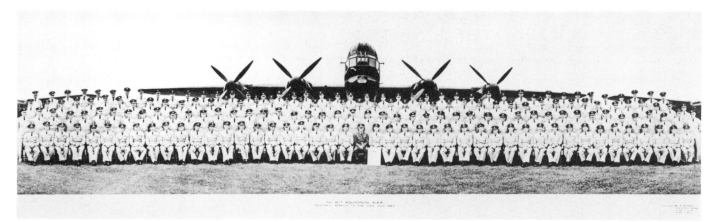

Overseas Tours

July 1947 saw a 'goodwill' tour of America and Canada by 617 who flew out in twelve aircraft on 1 August. The outward tour included flights to Boston, Baltimore, Reading, Philadelphia, New York, New Haven and Providence and returned via Bedford, Newark and Atlantic City. With a flypast over Detroit on 4 August and another over Chicago four days later, 617 was certainly kept busy. Three days later on 11 August they flew over the Rocky Mountains to Fresno via New Mexico and Arizona before landing at Mather Field, Sacramento. Continuing to San Francisco and Los Angeles, 617 then had a break from display flying with tours of the Hollywood film studios, Ling Beach naval yard where Hughes' Spruce Goose was being built, and meetings with film stars Nigel Bruce and Phyllis Calvert before flying to Abilene in Texas and on to Fort Worth. There the Squadron took the opportunity to visit the Vultee Aircraft Factory and saw the huge B-36 bomber under construction. 617 then flew to Mather Field in Alabama and laid wreaths on the graves of RAF flying trainees who had died in air accidents, before going on to Washington, DC on 25 August. Total flying time throughout the month was almost 600 hours, but almost immediately the Canadian tour began.

Although on a very much smaller scale, this tour involved flights to Trenton, Ontario and exhibition flights until 5 September when 617 flew to Gander, Newfoundland. With the fitting of long-range fuel tanks completed on 6 September, the Squadron took off and arrived back in Britain at 0520 on 9 September.

Top Left: Operation 'Goodwill', the American tour in 1947. A group photograph of all crews involved. (Author)

Left: 617 Squadron aircraft over Washington in 1947 during Operation 'Goodwill'. (Author)

Right: 617 Squadron en route to America overfly the liner Queen Elizabeth in the Atlantic. (Author)

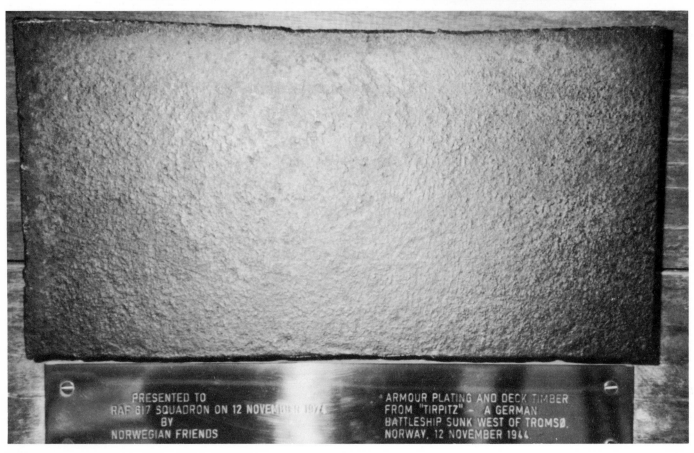

The Lincoln and Canberra Era

When Tirpitz was being broken up in the late 1940s an engine room bulkhead was found to have been adorned with an illustration of the ship accompanied by a U-boat steaming 'Gegen England' ('against England'). This was presented to the RAF in November 1949 by the Norwegian Government and accepted by the RAF Air Historical Branch. There now began more than 40 years of good-natured rivalry between 617 and 9 Squadrons who, both having flown on the Tirpitz raids, felt that the memorial bulkhead should remain with them. It presently resides at RAF Marham with 617 Squadron, having been 'lifted' from its wall-mounted display at 9 Squadron, RAF Bruggen in Germany by 617 personnel disguised as workmen!

Against this long-running entertainment 617 converted to the Avro Lincoln bomber and while flying it set a record during Operation 'Sunray'; the non-stop flight from Binbrook to Castel Binito in Egypt as part of the new Bomber Command commitment to the regular cycle of flights of six aircraft per month. During this period 617 Squadron competed for the Laurence Minot Trophy, a visual bombing contest in memory of Captain Minot who died in combat with 57 Squadron in 1917 and which the Air Council decided would be awarded for proficiency in bombing. Initially it went to the best individual crew, but from 1950 to the best overall squadron. 617 won it first with a margin of error of 120.9 yards. The Squadron received the trophy from The King on 8 November 1950, the ceremony taking place in the room in which Gibson and the Dambusters had received their post-raid medals seven years before.

Two years later 617 converted to the Canberra Light Bomber and were posted to RAF Butterworth in Malaya, a country involved in internal civil unrest against the British. On 1 August a morning strike of three aircraft took off for Operation 'Mileage', a bombing raid on the Mentakab area, each aircraft dropping three 1,000-pound bombs through cloud cover. Communist forces were later seen fleeing the area and the strike was adjudged successful. Again bombing targets on the Tapah Road the next day, 617 then flew an unusual mission on 5 August — an endurance flight in a B6 aircraft with wing-tip fuel tanks and no bomb load. Six days later disaster struck: a normal bombing raid.went seriously wrong when one aircraft released its load of six 1,000-pound bombs early and struck the datum point flare, killing three and injuring six ground troops. All Canberras were immediately grounded pending an inquiry which found the fault to lie in a short-circuit of the electrical bombing circuits. Three 617 officers laid wreaths at the funerals in Kuala Lumpur, and letters were sent to the next of kin. 617 returned home to Binbrook on 1 December 1955 and within two weeks was disbanded.

Top Left: The bulkhead from Tirpitz presented to Bomber Command by the Norwegian Government. This was then presented to 617 and 9 Squadrons to be shared as a trophy — 617 have it at present. (Author)

Left: A piece of armour plate from Tirpitz presented to 617 by Norwegian friends on 12 November 1974. (Author)

Above left: *The presentation of the Laurence Minot Trophy at Buckingham Palace by the King in 1950. (617 Squadron, Marham)*

Above: *617 march out of the Palace in 1950 having been presented with the Minot Trophy, awarded for the best bombing results in Bomber Command. (617 Squadron, Marham)*

Left: *The Minot Trophy in the centre with others won by 617: the Armaments Trophy (The Cock) is to the right and behind the 617 Squadron Standard with eight battle honours. (617 Squadron, Marham)*

Top right: *Canberras of 617 Squadron flying an operation in Malaya in 1955. (617 Squadron, Marham)*

Right: *Two Canberras at close quarters during an operation in Malaya. (617 Squadron, Marham)*

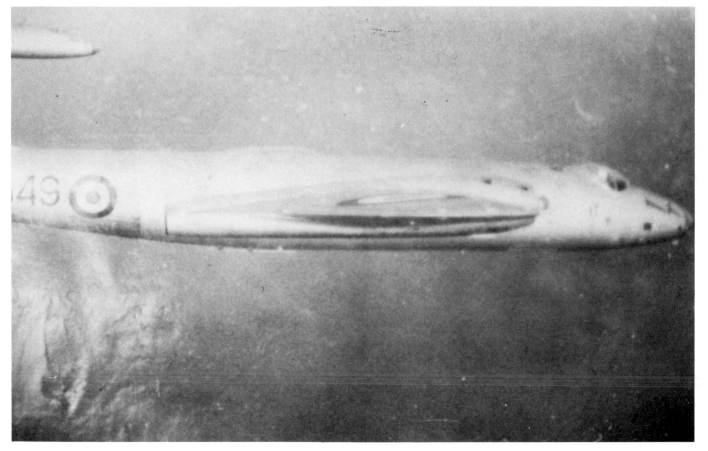

Left: A painting of a 617 Squadron Vulcan by Maurice Gardner, now in the Larmour Collection.

Left: The first Vulcan bomber, XH 482 1, delivered to 617 Squadron in May 1958. (D. Bower, RAF Scampton)

Left: Before the take-off for Goose Bay. Wing Commander Douglas Bower who was CO of 617 and Air Commodore Charles Whitworth, who had been the wartime station commander at RAF Scampton during the dams raid, can be seen. (D. Bower, RAF Scampton)

The Vulcan Era

On 1 May 1958 617 was reformed with the Avro Vulcan BI, the first Vulcan squadron equipped with the great delta-winged 4-jet bomber as part of the Medium Bomber Force, RAF. Returning to their old station of RAF Scampton, 617 collected their first aircraft the next day, Flight Lieutenant Thomas piloting Vulcan XH 482, accompanied by Group Captain Coulson from Scampton, the SASO of No 1 Group Air, Commodore Whitworth, and 617's Commanding Officer, Wing Commander Bower. On a cross-country navigational check flight on 16 May, XH 482, flown by Flight Lieutenant Streatfield, was featured by BBC TV that night.

The first weeks of April 1959 were spent in preparations for a visit to America and on 9 April three Vulcans commanded by AOC No 1 Group, Air Vice Marshal Walker, took off for Goose Bay en route for the World Air Congress of Flight at Las Vegas. All arrived at Nellis Airfield Goose Bay safely, but Squadron Leader Davenport, flying XH 500, hit a flock of birds and his aircraft's Nos 1 and 4 engines had to be replaced. He took no further part in the Air Congress and a replacement aircraft was sent out from Scampton.

On their return to Britain 617 were to be presented with a squadron Standard in May, the design having been approved more than seven years earlier. The Queen Mother continued her connections with 617 by making the presentation on a warm and sunny afternoon. The Squadron had rehearsed hard for the day and the ceremony took place at 1130 on the 14th between Nos 2 and 3 hangars, in the presence of more than 1,200 guests including Barnes Wallis, Group Captain Tait and Leonard Cheshire. A perfect fly-past was made by a Lancaster of 208 Canadian Squadron and three Vulcans of 83 Squadron as the RAF College Band played the theme from the film 'The Dambusters'. A display

of all aircraft flown by 617 from Lancaster to Vulcan was set up in No 3 hangar, all the types being armed with their appropriate bombs. Numerous photographs of 617 Squadron world-wide and a model of the Moehne dam were on display. At the celebratory party that night the subject of the *Tirpitz* bulkhead came up again and 9 Squadron once again was 'visited' by 617 and the memorial was 'borrowed.'

617 won the Minot Trophy again in 1959 as well as the Sasson Trophy. The latter had been set up in 1933 by the Under Secretary of State for Air as a contest in bombing skills but had been changed in 1953 to feature navigational proficiency. Another V squadron, 138 Squadron, flying Valiants, had won it in 1958. 617 made it three awards in one year with the Armament Officers Trophy, or 'The Cock'. The Squadron continued to set records throughout their time with the Vulcan; Squadron Leader Bearis making a non-stop flight from the United Kingdom to Australia in 1961. Flying XH 481, this first very long range air-refuelled flight in a Vulcan took 20 hours 3 minutes at an average speed of 573 miles per hour. 617 trained to deploy the new Blue Steel missile in 1963 when they again won the Sasson Trophy, and in 1969 won the British Siddeley Bombing Trophy to underline the excellence and high standards associated with this famous squadron. The end of the Vulcan era came on 31 December when 617 was disbanded again, pending the introduction into squadron service of the Panavia Tornado MRCA which was due in 1983. The last flight of the Vulcan with 617 came as Wing Commander Herbertson flew XL 318 over the Derwent and Bower dams in Derbyshire, where Gibson and his crews had trained nearly 40 years earlier. XL 318 was then dismantled and taken by road to the RAF Museum Hendon where she is now on display in the Bomber Command Hall of Fame.

Left: Before the Goose Bay take-off the crews have a final briefing. In the centre is Air Vice Marshal 'Gus' Walker who went as the detachment commander. At the time he was AOC No 1 Group. (D. Bower, RAF Scampton)

Left: The Las Vegas air display in April 1959. The Vulcans of 617 prepare to land. (Temple Press Ltd)

Left: Standard presentation in 1959. The Queen Mother inspects the line up of 617 Squadron. (D. Bower, RAF Scampton)

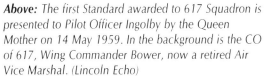

Above: *The first Standard awarded to 617 Squadron is presented to Pilot Officer Ingolby by the Queen Mother on 14 May 1959. In the background is the CO of 617, Wing Commander Bower, now a retired Air Vice Marshal. (Lincoln Echo)*

Top right: *The dais for the presentation of the Standard to 617 on 14 May 1959. Left to right: Air Vice Marshal Walker (AOC No 1 Group) and, on the dais with the Queen Mother, Air Chief Marshal Sir Harry Broadhurst (CinC Bomber Command). (RAF Marham)*

Centre right: *The Queen departs Scampton on 14 May 1959 after the presentation of the Standard. (D. Bower, RAF Scampton)*

Right: *The officers' mess at Scampton and the trophies won by 617. (D. Bower, RAF Scampton)*

Left: The Blue Steel bomb used by 617 Squadron in 1963. This specimen is now in the RAF Museum at Hendon. (Author)

Left: Squadron Leader Bearis and his record-breaking Vulcan crew. They flew to Australia in 20 hours 3 minutes via a mid air refuelling in 1961. (M. Bearis)

Left: The route flown by XH 481. (M. Bearis)

The Tornado Era

The Squadron was reformed on 1 January 1983 with the new title 617 Tornado Squadron, and was based at RAF Marham. Full strength was to be twelve Tornados under the command of Wing Commander Harrison, who believed the new aeroplane to be: 'A super aircraft — the best I have ever flown and we have chosen the aircrew to fly it with that in mind — the cream.'

Each Tornado cost in excess of £12 million, a far cry from the £20,000 needed for a Lancaster forty years earlier. A Tornado now costs more than £28 million, and it remains a formidable weapon and possesses a greater potential for destruction than a whole squadron of Lancasters. In 1988 the Squadron was presented with a new Standard and again the Queen Mother performed the ceremony.

A typical day in 617 at Marham begins at 0745 and lasts a minimum of ten hours. For a mission planned to start at 1530 the preparation begins up to two and a half hours beforehand with route planning, weather briefing and kitting-up all taking time and effort. Each morning there is an 0800 hours briefing by the Squadron Air Officer Administration which includes the vital UK weather scene, and it is probably the only time during the day that all flying personnel are together and can discuss flying topics. The day's scheduled sorties can be anything from a single aircraft mission to a five-aircraft formation flight. Sorties may involve liaison with 55 Squadron and their refuelling Victor aircraft and there are always exercises taking place abroad that need continual planning, such as the Chile Air Show where 617 Tornados were well received particularly due to a solo display by Squadron Leaders Riley and Anderson who served in the Gulf War.

At a fly-past earlier this year a third generation of Iveson family members were with 617, emphasizing the great traditions and loyalties that The Dambusters command. This fly-past was a normal exercise for the Squadron whose precision timing is vital to get all aircraft over the target in formation at the right time. Every member of the unit is a professional. All riggers, electricians, avionics experts (or 'fairies' as they are known), armourers (or 'plumbers') and administrative staff are highly trained individuals, working as part of an impressive team.

Outside the station there are the permanent reminders of why 617 is one of the most renowned and respected RAF squadrons; the Bouncing Bomb, Tallboy and Grand Slam sit next to a captured Iraqi AA gun as reminders of the reason for 617's existence.

Left: Flight Lieutenant Mark Jones plans his flight carefully. He only recently joined 617 after flying Canberras at RAF Wyton. (Author)

Right: Flying Officer Davies prepares for flight in the changing-rooms where all flying kit is stored. Around his neck he wears the modern equivalent of the Mae West. (Author)

Below left: Flying Officer Graeme Davies, navigator to Flight Lieutenant Jones, covers the route during the briefing for the day's flight. (Author)

Below: The ground crews at work on the Tornado prior to take-off. (Author)

Left: Tyres are checked before take-off by Corporal Evans, who served throughout the Gulf War. (Author)

Below: Jones taxies out of the 'house', the euphemism for the hangar, flying the only Gulf-coloured Tornado still in operation with 617 Squadron. (Author)

Right: The Queen Mother presents the second Standard to 617 in 1988. (RAF Marham)

Left: *The leading Tornado of a four-set due to make a fly-past over a passing-out parade at Cranwell, taxies out at Marham. (Author)*

Left: *The fly-past over Cranwell. (R. Berry)*

Left: *The six men of 617 Squadron who took part in the Chile Air Show in 1992: Bennett, Crook, Iveson, Youngman, Riley, Anderson. (RAF News)*

Right: Wing Commander Iveson, present OC 617, who in the Gulf commanded the TIALD Composite Squadron and completed ten missions. During the Falklands War in 1982 he flew Harriers and was shot down but evaded capture. In this photograph he is wearing the Falklands Medal with an Oak Leaf, indicating that he was mentioned in despatches. (R. Iveson)

Below: One of 617's recent visits was to the Chile Air Show where the Tornado was much admired. Here we see a 617 crew just after a display: the navigator was Flight Lieutenant Crook with Biggin Bear, a money-raising effort for the St John's Ambulance. (Richard Crook)

Left: The route of a pre-Gulf War Tornado crash: both crewmen ejected safely. (John Evans)

Left: The crashed Tornado. (John Evans)

Left: Flight Lieutenant Walker and his navigator, Flight Lieutenant Frost, in the Gulf. (G. Walker)

The Gulf War

The Iraqi invasion of Kuwait on 2 August 1990 took the world by surprise: King Fahd of neighbouring Saudi Arabia asked for help in defending his county and within 48 hours aircraft from Britain and America had landed in his country. Operation 'Granby' was under way.

NATO TACEVAL (Tactical Evaluation) Exercises had long demonstrated the RAF's ability to deploy aircraft quickly to trouble spots world-wide, and training in the UK had refined the process to a high level. For the Gulf War 617 Tornado Squadron became a Composite squadron, being joined with 27 Squadron both based at RAF Marham. The first Tornados flew to Muharraq in Bahrain on 19 September and went on to Tabuk on 8 October. All aircraft and aircrew were initially from RAF Laarbruch in Germany, but the composite unit involved seven crews from 617 and five crews from 27 Squadrons, all under the command of the Officer Commanding 14 Squadron. Two crews were sent on ahead to Tabuk to prepare for the remainder, and they were under the command of Wing Commander Iveson. Conditions at Tabuk were terrible; the base was only half built and the locals were hostile, resenting the arrival of noisy jet aircraft and the threat of war. For the other crews at Bahrain the reception was exactly the opposite; being a civil airport there was no option but to put squadron personnel into local hotels. Few complained.

The groundcrews were living and working from tents, prefabs not being erected until later, and it was they who experienced the discomforts of desert life the most keenly. Their main problem was the frequent and sudden occurrence of sandstorms: face masks and goggles were vital and all flying was suspended. Sand ingested into a jet engine crystallized on fan blades and timely repair work was necessary before flying could recommence. Although conditions were primitive, the absence of the flying restrictions imposed in the United Kingdom meant that the aircrews reached a standard of training impossible to achieve at home and thus they were well prepared for operational flying.

When it became obvious that Iraq was going to ignore the UN resolution calling for their withdrawal from Kuwait a final ultimatum was presented on 15 January 1991. Airpower was going to be the critical element in Allied planning. The Iraqi Air Force numbered in excess of 700 aircraft, some of these being the very latest in Soviet technology, so the Iraqis were by no means an enemy to be underrated, and the Allies devised a three-stage assault against Iraq with control of the air being the important prerequisite for a successful outcome. The air war began early on the morning of 17 January 1991 and was planned to embrace three distinct phases. One: To attack and destroy Iraqi airfields and aircraft; Two: To turn the weight of attack against Iraqi Ground Forces; Three: To support the land offensive to clear Kuwait.

Phase One airfield attacks were carried out at night by low-level Tornados armed with the JP233 Area Denial Weapon. This munition required a fast approach at 150-200 feet; any higher risked losing accuracy, any lower risked malfunction of the delaying parachute and failure of the bomb. These missions were to suffer the highest loss rate for any Coalition aircraft; Flying Officer Mark Youngman records his impressions of such a mission:

'Have you ever seen anything like that in your life [AA fire] ... there is a big explosion on the airport, the airport is going up, I think that was a crash ... Oh God!'

He had just seen the first Tornado shot down during the war. Mark knew that low-level night ops over heavily defended airfields would be part of his job and would be risky, but:

'I became more flexible. It is difficult to explain what it is like in combat. The best thing in any war is to send someone else.'

He goes on to describe how 617 chose to attack their target airfields, and how experience shaped their tactics:

'To attack a runway only 50 yards long by 50 wide meant the margin of error was very small, so we ended up flying at an angle to the target of anything between 10 and

90 degrees. This way there was a better chance of getting three or even four ships across than on a straight or frontal attack. In this angle you were exposed to fire for perhaps 15 seconds whereas in a front attack it was more like 25 seconds. Even allowing for the greater part of the Iraqis being conscripts, flying at that height there was a good chance you'd get hit.'

When Flight Lieutenants Walker and Frost first saw AA fire coming up at them they likened it to a torch flashing and then waiting for an explosion. Their first mission was their most worrying as no one fired at them. After only three days the air war switched to Phase Two and the targets became medium-altitude attacks on precision targets such as bridges, bunkers and weapons sites. Although this generally removed the threat of AA fire the crews were still vulnerable to guided missiles. These initial mid-level attacks were carried out using 'Smart Bombs' in the 'lofted' bombing technique whereby on approach the aircraft's nose was lifted so that the bomb was `lofted' on to the target.

Later missions were flown with the TIALD (Thermal Imaging Airborne Laser Designator) Pod fitted, and this was fully integrated with the Tornado's own navigation and bombing systems following rushed trials by 13 Squadron at Boscombe Down. The display in the Tornado gave an infra-red image of the target as seen by the weapon and once engaged and locked, TIALD kept the weapon fully trained on to the target regardless of any evasive action the aircraft might have to take.

One crew always carried a bible in their aircraft. It had been sent to them by an ex-wartime member of 617 who had always had it with him on ops. Another crew christened

their Tornado 'AJ' after the pilot's wife, Amanda Jane, who had given birth to a daughter; despite being ordered back to the UK, the pilot remained to complete eleven missions. Although crews were aware that the Iraqi Air Force was all but beaten, many still kept an anxious eye over their shoulder when flying, and the television reports that downed crews were alive as prisoners went a long way to restoring morale.

Each crew also carried a personal survival pack which included condoms for carrying water and tampons for lighting fires at night! Once accustomed to the prevailing conditions, 617 Squadron felt that they could stay in the Gulf for months if needed, but only because operating procedures had been kept simple and had been found to work. As Wing Commander Iveson concluded:

'The war was decided and won in the air: the Iraqi Army was beaten from the air. The tension came when you saw the border approaching: although it was only a line on a map you knew that as soon as you crossed it things would start to happen. No longer was this an exercise; there were people down there who were ready to launch real missiles at you.'

On 21 June 1991 there was a victory parade in London for the servicemen returning from the Gulf War. The weather was terrible and the planned grand fly-past was a greatly reduced affair: Iveson led four Tornados in a box formation, two from 617 and two from 27 Squadrons across the capital. The Gulf War had shown that the defence of Britain was in good hands after the display of skill and expertise by the RAF and 617 Squadron in particular.

Right: An Iraqi airfield as seen by Flight Lieutenant Walker in his aircraft. (G. Walker)

Right: All 617 aircraft in the Gulf displayed 'nose art'. In this case 'Foxy Killer' has completed several missions. (John Evans)

Left: A low-level sortie during the build-up period pre-war, taken by the navigator in a Tornado. (P. Wharmby)

Right: The groundcrew rest between missions. (John Evans)

Top Left: A party of 617 Squadron groundcrew in the Gulf: 'Foxy Killer' is in the background. (John Evans)

Above: The armaments carried by 617 Tornados in the Gulf: this example was delivered by Corporal Evans who inscribed the message 'From Betty's Chip Shop'. (John Evans)

Left: ZD 851-AJ Amanda Jane and ZD 850-CL Cherry Lips. AJ were the squadron letters throughout the Second World War. (Maurice Gardner)

Left: Debbie returning from a sortie over Iraq. (P. Wharmby)

Above: 617 Squadron hear that the Gulf War is over. (G. Walker)

Below: Flight Lieutenant Walker is greeted by his wife and child on his return from the Gulf. (G. Walker)

Left: The Dambusters film reception. Left to right: Percy Pigeon, Wally Dunn, Michael Anderson and Brian Goodale. (Wally Dunn)

Left: On the set at Elstree studios during the making of the film. Left to right: Wally Dunn, Michael Redgrave and Mrs Dunn. (Wally Dunn)

Left: At the première of the film at The Odeon Leicester Square in 1955. Richard Todd talks to Charles and Mrs Franklin. (Mrs Franklin)

Reunions

Over the years there have been many squadron reunions mostly organized by 617 Squadron Association, the patron of which was Sir Barnes Wallis until his death in 1979.

From a 1951 book came a film in 1955. 'The Dambusters' starred Richard Todd as Guy Gibson and Michael Redgrave as Barnes Wallis. It had taken more than two years to research at a cost of £250,000. Wing Commander Wally Dunn, who had taken down the signal that the Moehne dam had been breached in 1943, was appointed Technical Adviser and it was he who dubbed the Morse Code signals on to the famous soundtrack of the film. Most of the flying scenes were shot around the Derwent Lake reservoir in Sheffield. Although this was 1953, the Bouncing Bomb was still on the Air Ministry's secret list so the bomb seen in the film is more like a large beach ball than a drum as it should have been. Gibson's dog Nigger was faithfully portrayed by an army dog who faltered only once: when required to go to the real Nigger's grave he flatly refused. The three Lancasters seen in the film had been brought out of retirement at Aston and converted to Dambuster-type aircraft at a cost of £3,000. A special premiere of the film took place on 16/17 May 1955 at the Empire Leicester Square, with a reception afterwards at The Criterion in Regent Street where a 9-foot by 3-foot model of the dams was on display.

In 1974, to commemorate the 50th anniversary of the founding of the Observer Corps, a bouncing bomb, made of pieces recovered from the Ashley Walk ranges, was presented to 617 Squadron and it remains today as gate guardian at RAF Scampton. In 1976, the 617 reunion was in Holland and the party visited the graves of Gibson and his navigator Warwick, and unveiled a small memorial there.

On the 90th birthday of Barnes Wallis on 26 September 1977, a special fly-past by a Vulcan of 617 Squadron was arranged to pass over his home in Effingham, a white sheet and a yellow towel being used to guide the bomber in! In April 1980, the 617 reunion was in Australia where they led the Anzac parade, and a commemorative tree was planted at Adelaide Airport. A second reunion was held on 16/17 May at the Rolls-Royce works in Derby.

In 1983, the 40th anniversary of Operation 'Chastise' saw the reunion being held in the Lincoln area with a base at the Petwood Hotel, Woodhall Spa.

Outside the hotel there is still a bouncing bomb, although it is now a little the worse for wear, and the RAF ensign flies on the flagpole as it did when the hotel was the officers' mess for 617 and 619 Squadrons. In 1987, a memorial was unveiled in the Royal Square Gardens in Woodhall to those men of 617 who died during the Second World War. There are to date 201 names on the memorial.

A strange incident happened after the ceremony: the choir was having a photograph taken when from nowhere a black dog remarkably similar to Nigger appeared and sat down in the middle of the group. Afterwards it promptly disappeared; it had never been seen before nor has anyone seen it since. In 1988, sixty-four veterans met at the Derwent dam —eleven of them had flown on the dams raid — to witness a fly-past of the Lancaster from the Battle of Britain Memorial Flight. It flew in over the lake at the appropriate height of 60 feet in salute to all those who never returned from the war. The Second World War is an inextricable part of 20th-century history, but its veterans dwindle in number as the years go by. Yet the Dambusters raid continues to excite the imagination of people who had not been born when Operation 'Chastise' took place. The memory of those brave men who flew into the heart of Germany in 1943 lives on.

On 27 August 1992, exactly two years since the trouble in the Gulf flared up, the placards for the early editions of the evening paper in London said 'Dam Busters Fly Back to Iraq'. Their role on this occasion was to enforce a multinational air exclusion zone over southern Iraq under the code-name Operation 'Jural'.

Three of the composite squadron of six sent out to Dhahran were from 617 Squadron, led by their commanding officer, Wing Commander Bob Iveson, who had commanded the TIALD Squadron during the Gulf war; his navigator, Squadron Leader Bobby Anderson, had also served in the Gulf conflict and was obliged to eject from his aircraft on one occasion. One of the other 617 Tornados was flown by Flight Lieutenant Gareth Walker, also a Gulf veteran.

After a wet take-off from RAF Marham in the early hours of the 27th, they arrived in Dhahran at 3.10 p.m., having been refuelled en route by a VC10 tanker from Brize Norton and later by an RAF Tristar.

Once they had landed, the groundcrew under Warrant Officer Dave Goodlad, who had arrived by Hercules, had the task — in temperatures of 100 degrees plus — of fitting the TIALD pods and making sure they were working. Once up and running, the crews were flying two missions a day, and the video pictures from the early missions were described as 'magic'.

Barnes Wallis

Above: Barnes Wallis receives a 90th birthday fly-past from a 617 Vulcan. (B. Wallis)

Opposite page, top left: The poster advertising the film. (Author)

Opposite page, top right: Barnes Wallis explaining the workings of his bouncing bomb before the exhibit at the RAF Museum, Hendon. (MoD)

Right: A reunion in Australia in 1980. Left centre is Willie Tait and centre right Leonard Cheshire. (Bill Howarth)

Left: *The 617 memorial at Woodhall Spa unveiled in 1987. It had 201 names of the men of 617 Squadron who were killed during the Second World War. In the centre the unknown dog who resembles Nigger. (Mark Upton)*

Opposite page, bottom left: *Les Sumpter, a bomb-aimer on the dams raid, meets the man who would have been trying to shoot him down when attacking the Moehne: Karl Schutte who was a flak gunner on the dam in 1943. This meeting in 1989 is in a more peaceful setting: Sumpter, Author, Schutte. (Hilda Cooper)*

Opposite page, bottom right: *Karl Schutte is re-decorated with his Iron Cross by the author on the Moehne dam in 1989. (Hilda Cooper)*

Below: *A reunion on the Moehne dam as members of 617 Association line up where the breach was made fifty years before. (D. Warren)*

Right: *The Eder dam today, with the famous Waldeck Castle in the background. (Author)*

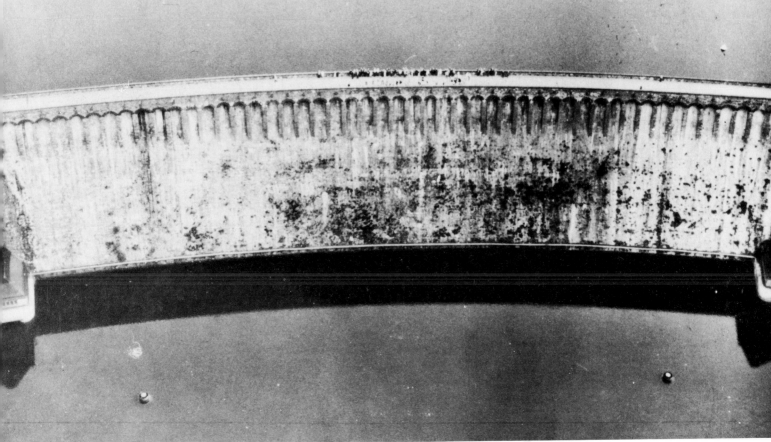

Left: The last photograph of Barnes Wallis before he died in 1978: taken by the author at Wallis' home in Effingham. (Author)

Left: A pictorial covering the history of 617 in the Squadron Bar at the Petwood Hotel. (Author)

Left: Len Sumpter pays homage to the men of 617 at the Reichswald War Cemetery in 1989. (Hilda Cooper)